AIRCAM /**AIRWAR**   EDITOR: MARTIN WINDROW

RAF FIGHTER UNITS
EUROPE APRIL 1942-45

BY BRYAN PHILPOTT

COLOUR PLATES BY
MICHAEL ROFFE
AND GERRY EMBLETON

OSPREY PUBLISHING LONDON

Published in 1978 by
Osprey Publishing Ltd
Member company of the George Philip Group
12–14 Long Acre, London WC2E 9LP
© Copyright 1978 Osprey Publishing Ltd

ISBN 0 85045 233 3

Filmset by BAS Printers Limited, Over Wallop, Hampshire

Printed in Hong Kong

I should like to acknowledge the help given by the following,
Richard Leask Ward, Mac Kennaugh, Christopher Brown,
Peter Carpenter, Flt Lt Eric Bailey, the staff of the Imperial
War Museum, Mr C. G. Taft of Coles Cranes Limited and Mrs
Christine Williams.

ON THE OFFENSIVE

Under the leadership of its new Commander-in-Chief, Air Marshal Sholto Douglas, Fighter Command, although keeping a high defensive commitment, had been on the offensive since January 1941. This situation suited the C-in-C, who was a man far happier when he was able to adopt an aggressive, rather than passive role; in this he was ably supported by the commander of No. 11 Group, Air Vice Marshal Trafford Leigh-Mallory, who for months had been championing the use of large formations of fighters in wing rather than squadron strength.

Although Leigh-Mallory's ideas had been aired at great length during the Battle of Britain, bringing friction between him and the commander of No. 11 Group, Air Vice Marshal Keith Park, they had never been brought to fruition in the way he envisaged them. But in February 1941, with Fighter Command in a position to strike back at the enemy, the Wing System was adopted, the first two being the Biggin Hill and Tangmere Wings, led respectively by Wg Cdr A. G. Malan and Wg Cdr D. R. S. Bader.

Each wing comprised three or four squadrons and was very similar to the *Gruppe* organization adopted by the Luftwaffe. Apart from isolated occasions during the Battle of Britain, wings had proved too unwieldy for defensive purposes, where time to form-up was not always on the side of the defenders. But, as a method of carrying the fight to the enemy in his airspace, where numerical inferiority would be a grave disadvantage, they were to become an ideal method of fighter concentration.

The offensive against Europe was aimed at achieving air superiority over Northern France and gaining complete control of the air over the Channel, thus paving the way for an invasion, which in 1941 was still a long way off. To do this, Fighter Command adopted several types of attack, each with a code name: a *Rhubarb* was a small-scale attack by fighters or fighter-bombers against ground targets; sometimes the target was defined but more often than not pairs of aircraft entered enemy airspace and attacked targets of opportunity; a *Circus* was a daylight attack by heavily escorted light bombers aimed at specific targets within the fighters' operational range, with the prime purpose of bringing enemy fighters into action, thereby forcing the Luftwaffe into maintaining a strong defensive force in the area concerned; a *Ramrod* was a straightforward escort operation in some ways similar to a *Circus* but with the objective being the destruction of the bombers' target rather than using them as bait to attract enemy fighters; a *Roadstead* was an operation aimed at enemy shipping either at sea or in harbour mounted by fighters or light bombers escorted by fighters; a *Rodeo* was purely a fighter sweep over enemy territory and, finally, a *Ranger* was an operation at wing or group strength allowing free-lance intrusion with the sole purpose of wearing down defenders. There were other types of sortie, such as a *Rover* which was armed reconnaissance behind enemy lines, but those mentioned in detail were the main elements of the command's planning when the offensive started. The first *Circus* was carried out in January 1941 when three Hurricane and six Spitfire squadrons escorted Blenheims against targets in the Pas de Calais area, the gain being little more than a morale booster for the crews and the beleagured British public.

From June to October, when the onset of winter curtailed operations, Fighter Command maintained as much pressure as it could, but the growing efficiency of the Luftwaffe fighter control organization in France, plus the limited range of the RAF fighters involved, brought about a situation where-

1. Lt Gen H. C. Lloyd inspects Mustangs and personnel of No. 170 Sqn at RAF Andover on 9 November 1942. At that time, a number of Mustang units were assigned to army support duties, the early Allison-engined machines being part of Army Co-operation Command. These aircraft bore the appropriate badge of their 'parent' ground formation and the insignia of the Guards Armoured Division can be seen on the two aircraft visible here. (IWM)

by the RAF was losing more aircraft and pilots than the Luftwaffe.

At this time the main equipment of the opposing forces was fairly equally matched, with the RAF using the latest Mk V Spitfire and the Luftwaffe the Bf109F-2. This equality of equipment lasted until July 1941 when the new Fw190 started to arrive in France to give the Luftwaffe a distinct advantage over the Spitfire V. But the full effect of this advantage was not realized until early 1942, for although the Fw190 had encountered the Spitfire in combat during September 1941, reports of its existence by RAF pilots had been dismissed by Air Intelligence, who believed them to be obsolete Curtiss Hawk fighters captured from the French.

The Fw190 arrived in the combat zone in July 1941, when it was issued to 6/JG 26 commanded by *Oberleutnant* Walter Schneider, to replace obsolescent Bf109E-7s. Initial teething troubles with the aircraft's cooling system did not exactly endear the '190 to the German pilots, but by September these problems had been solved and the whole of II/JG 26 was equipped with the aircraft, which was superior in every respect to the Spitfire Vb. One criticism the pilots had of their new mount was its armament, which was inferior to that carried by the Bf109F-4, but the introduction of the A-2 model with an improved BMW 801 engine, two fuselage mounted MG 17 machine guns, and two wing mounted 20mm MG 151 cannon, brought more favourable comments. Initial operations, which had started in August, were disappointing, 6/JG 26 losing three of its experienced pilots in a ten day period, followed by the loss of the *Gruppenkommandeur, Hauptmann* Walter Adolph, on 18 September. Operational losses and accidents, one of which claimed the life of *Oberleutnant* Schneider, *Staffelkapitän* of 6/JG 26, gave the Fw190 an inauspicious start to its career, but as 1942 opened, there was much greater confidence in the aircraft. Only a major success in combat was needed to confirm the pilots' views that it would be more than a match for their adversaries.

This success was not long in coming, for on 12 February, JG 2 and JG 26 provided fighter cover for the Channel dash of the capital ships *Scharnhorst*, *Prince Eugen* and *Gneisnau*, during which the RAF and FAA lost twenty bombers, six torpedo-bombers and sixteen fighters, against the Luftwaffe's eleven fighters, three of which were Fw190s. (see *RAF Fighter Units 1939–42*). The two *Jagdgeschwader* involved in the defence of the trio of German warships were in fact, the sole elements of the Luftwaffe fighter arm left in France after the invasion of Russia in June 1941. Their strength rarely rose above 250 serviceable aircraft and at one time, when 7 *Staffel* of III/JG 26 was detached to the Mediterranean, it was as low as 144. But the units were at least fighting from a position of strength, operating over their own territory, against RAF fighters which were faced with a haul across the Channel and limited time in the combat zone. This was indeed a reversal of roles, since the Luftwaffe fighter elements had had exactly the same problems themselves during the operations over England the previous summer.

The continuing assaults by Fighter Command eventually achieved the desired effect of forcing the Luftwaffe to re-strengthen its fighter force in the west, but this was still some way off in 1942, and in the final reckoning, proved to be a very costly business, both in terms of loss of aircraft and pilots. In March 1942, Fighter Command resumed its offensive, which in the winter months, had been severely curtailed by inclement weather. Although on occasions, bad weather was ideal for fighter interdiction, it had made bomber operations impossible. Nonetheless, fighter sweeps had continued, keeping the Luftwaffe and ground defences on their toes. Flak proved particularly effective against low flying fighters and among RAF losses was Wg Cdr Bob Stanford-Tuck, the Biggin Hill wing leader, who was shot down by ground fire on 28 January. The loss of this popular leader, who at the time had only just returned from a lecture tour in the USA, was a severe blow to the wing and a considerable morale booster to the enemy. Wg Cdr Michael Lister-Robinson took over from Tuck, but this equally-popular former CO of No. 609 Squadron was killed in combat with II/JG 26 over Le Touquet on 10 April, barely a month after the start of the renewed offensive.

The efficiency of the *Jagdgruppen* defending the coast from Leeuwarden in Holland to Brest in France

2. Sqn Ldr J. A. F. Maclachlan, the one-armed CO of No. 1 Sqn poses in front of his Hurricane Mk IIc with his personal insignia, an embellishment that needs absolutely no explanation! Maclachlan lost his left arm in combat over Malta and went on to become a successful intruder pilot on Hurricanes. (IWM)

3. A Typhoon Mk Ib, of No. 486 (New Zealand) Sqn with the early 'car door' type cockpit and identification stripes under the wings. (Via R. L. Ward)

4. An immaculate Spitfire Mk IXc, BS459 of No. 306 (Polish) Sqn at Northolt. From the autumn of 1942 No. 306 was one of the four Spitfire units in No. 1 Polish Fighter Wing and flew many cross-Channel sweeps to targets in France and Belgium. (IWM)

was increasing daily with the result that in March, Fighter Command lost 32 Spitfires with a further 23 damaged, an attrition rate that increased to 103 Spitfires and one Hurricane in April. This success was due not only to the Fw190 but also to the establishment of an effective *Freya* and *Würzburg* early-warning radar chain along the coastline. *Freya* could track a target flying at 1,000 feet at a range of 56 miles; above 5,000 feet the range was nearly double. So at points along the Channel coast German radar was quite capable of picking up the British fighters as they formed up into their wing formations. Coupled to this, the large dish aerial of the *Würzburg*, although not having the range of the *Freya*, could accurately pin-point altitude. The intention of fighters and bombers forming up in shallow climbing turns over a selected rendezvous before setting course for their selected target could

therefore be monitored by the German ground controllers enabling them to get their defending fighters into a tactically favourable position.

Feints and diversionary sweeps helped to confuse the ground controllers, but it did not take an experienced operator too long to identify the build-up of a *Circus* as opposed to a low-level *Rhubarb*. Techniques adopted by Fighter Command to combat the early warning system were typical of those used by No. 72 Squadron on 23 April when it carried out a diversionary sweep over Abbeville whilst Bostons raided Ostend and Le Havre. The Spitfires stayed below 500 feet as they dashed across the Channel, then, on approaching the French coast, climbed as hard as they could to obtain as much altitude as possible over the German fighters that had scrambled to meet them. On this occasion the tactics worked, with No. 72 Squadron claiming four aircraft destroyed for the loss of two of its own number. But the dangers involved, especially on the return dash, by which time the enemy had gained height and had a fuel advantage, were graphically illustrated by Sgt Hughes. His Spitfire was chased

across the Channel by two Bf109s, which succeeded in damaging its radio, hydraulics and instruments as well as putting a neat groove in the sergeant's helmet.

5. Capt Horbaczewski (second left) CO of No. 315 (Polish) Sqn poses with his Mustang III and fellow pilots shortly before his death in 1944. The impressive scoreboard of the Mustang includes four V1 symbols, 13½ enemy aircraft shot down and 27 bomb symbols indicating ground-attack sorties. (IWM)

THE LONE INTRUDERS

The increasing offensive was not confined to daylight operations for, under cover of darkness, intruder sorties over enemy airfields, started in 1941, gathered momentum. The prolonged loiter time of twins such as the Blenheim, Havoc and Mosquito (now appearing in increasing numbers) made them ideal for this type of work, but alongside them there appeared an equally formidable weapon in the form of the Hurricane IIc. In the right hands, this stalwart of the Battle of Britain, now armed with four cannon and adapted to carry bombs or long range tanks, was capable of causing considerable havoc in the night skies.

A notable exponent of the art of night intruding was Sgt Karel Kuttelwascher of No. 1 Squadron, which was part of the Tangmere Wing. Kut-telwascher was a Czech who fled to England via the French Foreign Legion and the *Armee de l'Air* in June 1940 and joined No. 1 Squadron in July. By April 1941 he had been commissioned and began his long line of successes on the 8th, when he shot down a Bf109 during a daylight sweep over France. Very much a 'loner', Kuttelwascher immediately took to the individualism of night fighting and intruding, and when No. 1 Squadron moved to Tangmere in July 1941 to concentrate on such work, he was in his element. By April 1942, he was a flight commander and on the first day of that month gained the squadron's first night intruder victory. Taking off at 22.15 hrs with his Commanding Officer, Sqn Ldr James Maclachlan, a one-armed veteran of the Battle of France and Malta, Kut-telwascher made for the airfield at Evreux, where he

6. A Mustang III, FZ149 of No. 306 (Polish) Sqn. The aircraft has a Malcolm canopy and is plugged into its starter trolley ready to go at a moment's notice. The squadron was used for anti *Diver* (flying bomb) patrols over southern England in 1944. (IWM)

orbited at 3,000 feet for some time in the hope of finding returning bombers. His luck was out; so he flew on to Melun, where he found the flare path illuminated and a Junkers 88 ready for take-off. Keeping his eye on the enemy bomber, Kuttelwascher manoeuvred his Hurricane into a position from which he could follow it into the circuit. A flare indicated that the Ju88 pilot had been given take-off clearance, and soon the lurking Hurricane pilot could see navigation lights tracing the path of the aircraft down the runway.

The Ju88 climbed to 2,000 feet and turned downwind, with Kuttelwascher closing to 100 yards before opening fire. At that range the impact from the 20mm cannon shells was decisive and dramatic; the unfortunate German crew never knew what hit them as the starboard wing of their aircraft collapsed and it rolled over to plunge into the ground. Before the startled ground defences realized what had happened, Kuttelwascher made a low pass down the runway, strafing another Ju88 before pulling his Hurricane into a climbing turn and heading back to Tangmere.

On the third night of April, the Czech pilot claimed a Dornier 217 as a probable, then on 16 April shot down another of the same type as it made its final approach into St Andre airfield. Other squadron pilots did not meet with the same success

as Kuttelwascher, although on 26 April Maclachlan opened his account with a Do217, an event which started an unofficial competition between the two men. The night of 4/5 May saw Maclachlan in action over Dinard, where he destroyed a Do217 and a He111 within a few minutes of each other. Not to be outdone, Kuttelwascher broke all previous records by claiming three victories in one evening over his favourite hunting ground at St Andre. Joining the circuit behind six He111s at 1,500 feet, the Hurricane pilot had a moment of apprehension when three searchlights flickered up at him, but a flash from his navigation lights saw these doused and left him free to concentrate on the work in hand. A short burst from his lethal cannon saw the last Heinkel in the procession of six plunge to earth, soon to be followed by the fifth, which disintegrated into a flaming ball. The other four flew serenely on, unaware of the fate of their comrades, so Kuttelwascher moved up the line and destroyed his third victim of the night. By this time, those on the ground had awoken to the fact that an intruder was present, the lights were extinguished and a barrage of light flak was put up in the general direction of the Hurricane. Not wishing to tempt fate, Kuttelwascher returned to Tangmere, well satisfied with his evening's work.

Intruder operations, the success of which relied on basic cunning plus an inbuilt hunting instinct, continued throughout the summer, with railway locomotives and other ground targets proving as attractive bait as Luftwaffe bombers. In the meantime daylight operations continued apace with

7. The pilot and navigator of this intruder Mosquito are wearing late-style Mae West life-jackets, oxygen masks and helmets. The pilot (left) sports a silk scarf in traditional fighter pilot fashion, which was not an intentional flaunt of regulations, but a functional item of dress, as it prevented chafing of the neck when the head was continually turned in the essential watch for enemy aircraft. (Author's collection)

8. The same Mosquito crew shown previously with contrasting styles in flying boots. At left, the pilot wears the escape-type boot with suede fur-lined uppers and leather shoe-type soles, while the navigator has suede fur-lined boots. (Author's collection)

9. Spitfire Mk IXc aircraft of No. 34 (Belgian) Sqn taxi to dispersal at Friston in Arctic conditions during February 1944, a few days before joining 2nd TAF.

10. The sting of the Mosquito. Four machine guns and a quartet of cannon, fitted to a superb aircraft, made a devastating weapon. Here, the variant is an FB IV. (Via R. L. Ward)

RAF pilots trying their best to combat the Fw190 with outclassed equipment and suffering severely when the German fighter was met in any strength. An aura of invincibility was building up around the Fw190 and events of 1 June 1942 serve to illustrate the reason for this. It was a typically English summer day with scattered cloud at 8,000 and 25,000 feet; at 10.30 hrs the Biggin Hill and North Weald Wings had set off on a *Rodeo* to tempt the Luftwaffe fighters into the air, and engage them in combat so that the Fw190s would be back on the ground being armed and re-fuelled when a *Circus* was mounted against lock gates on the canal at Bruges. This ruse failed, as the German controller kept his fighters on the ground, possibly having correctly concluded that the *Rodeo* was merely a diversion.

The *Circus* was undertaken by Hurricane IIB fighter-bombers of No. 174 Squadron, with a close escort of 33 Spitfires from the Hornchurch Wing, these in turn being covered by a further 48 from the Biggin Hill Wing and supported by a similar number from the Debden Wing. In the meantime 36 Spitfires from Kenley created a diversion. The escorting fighters met up with their charges over Eastchurch and with the Hornchurch Wing under Wg Cdr R. Powell staying close to the Hurricanes, the formation set off towards its target. The Debden Wing, which comprised Nos. 71, 350, 111 and 65 Squadrons, was covering the target area with No. 65 Squadron forming the lower echelon at 20,000 feet and No. 350 Squadron top cover at 25,000 feet. Over Bruges the Hurricanes, which together with their escorts had crossed the Channel at low level before pulling up to 10,000 feet to attack their target, made their run without loss in spite of the barrage of flak put up by the defence, and made a safe low-level get-away. The German controller scrambled III/JG 26 under the command of *Major* Josef 'Pips' Priller, and the Fw190s climbed at full throttle to join-up with *Hauptmann* Sifert's 1/JG 26, which was also flying '190s.

At 30,000 feet the German formation turned to attack the Debden Wing, 12 of them feinting at the middle echelon of No. 111 Squadron. The British aircraft turned to meet the threat, quickly realized that it was a feint as the '190s turned away and tried to regain their defensive composure. But the slight turn had been enough to disrupt the tightly-knit formation and No. 111 Squadron bore the brunt of the main attack. No. 71 'Eagle' Squadron, flying just above No. 111 Squadron, was immediately committed to the assistance of the lower echelon squadrons. No. 71's leader, Sqn Ldr G. Peterson flying Spitfire BL449, fired at two Fw190s, claiming one destroyed (a claim that was later proved to be incorrect), before his Spitfire had a large hole blown in it; Fg Off G. Daymond's section was set upon by three '190s which quickly accounted for his No. 2,

Plt Off G. Teicheira, leaving the American pilot in the unenviable position of engaging five '190s alone. After a prolonged combat followed by a chase in which Daymond saw cannon fire from his Spitfire strike one of his antagonists, he extricated himself from the mêlée and returned to Manston with barely enough fuel left to wet the tanks. No. 350 Squadron fared little better, being bounced by '190s as it tried to provide top cover, and lost Plt Off Laumans, F/Sgt Livyns, and Sgt Hansez, as well as Plt Off Richards, who baled out over the sea. Sgt Kopecek was badly wounded by the Fw190 which had accounted for Richards, but managed to crash-land at Manston. In addition to these pilots, the wing also lost Wg Cdr J. Gordon, Sergeants

11–12. Land targets were not the only objectives of Fighter Command aircraft in 1942–43. These two pictures show a naval vessel and a U-boat under attack by Mosquito FB VIs in the Kattegat during a typical anti-shipping *Roadstead*. (Via R. L. Ward)

Parrack, Bryson and Cummings, as well as having several aircraft severely damaged. A number of claims were made by the RAF pilots but Luftwaffe records for the day show that all Fw190s engaged returned safely to their bases. The following day, the North Weald and Hornchurch Wings, whilst carrying out a fighter sweep, suffered a similar

13. Mosquito NF XII, HK382, RO-T of No. 29 Squadron at dispersal at West Malling waiting for the night's work to begin. (IWM)

14. RAF Servicing Commandoes swarm round one of the first Spitfire Mk IXs to land in France after D-Day. The aircraft is being refuelled by hand; the cans under the wing are handed to the crew on the fuselage who are using a giant-sized funnel to direct the liquid into the right place. (IWM)

experience with No. 403 Squadron flying as top cover at 27,000 feet losing eight aircraft and six pilots. In his book *Nine Lives*, Alan Deere, who was CO of No. 403 Squadron at the time, says of the Fw190s, 'In Messerschmitt 109s the Hun tactics had always followed the same pattern—a quick pass and away, sound tactics against Spitfires with their

15. Landing strips in advanced areas were often laid using PBS—Prefabricated Bitumised Strips—over which went sections of perforated metal. A Coles Crane helps to stack PBS in a storage depot in France. (IWM)

superior turning circle. Not so these Fw190 pilots, they were full of confidence.' Confidence was the key word. After its initial troubles, the radial-engined German fighter was rapidly endearing itself to its pilots, not only because they knew and had proved that it was superior to the Spitfire V, but also because of its superb handling qualities and ability to accept much more damage than the Bf109 and still keep flying.

The RAF desperately needed two things to counter the advantage which had now moved into the Luftwaffe's hands. One was new fighters, the other an Fw190 to evaluate in the hope of finding weaknesses which could be exploited, until such time as it could be met on an equal footing. The former was on the way in the shape of the Spitfire Mk IX and the Typhoon, but the latter seemed an impossible pipe-dream. Whilst steps were being taken to marry the new Merlin 61 engine to the Mk V airframe to produce what many considered to be the best Spitfire of them all, plans were also afoot to mount a daring commando raid on a German airfield to capture an Fw190. Jeffery Quill, the Vickers test pilot, was to accompany the commandos who would attempt to counter enemy resistance whilst he gained access to an aircraft and flew it back to England. But on 23 June 1942, all the planning of the raid was negated—one suspects much to the relief of all the participants, especially Quill—by a simple navigation error on the part of *Oberleutnant* Arnim Faber, the adjutant of III/JG 2. Becoming disorientated after combat with Spitfires from the Exeter Wing, one of which (from No. 312 Squadron) he had shot down, Faber mistook the Bristol Channel for the English Channel and, low on fuel, landed at what he thought was a forward Luftwaffe airfield; it was in fact RAF Pembrey. The RAF thus gained a new and undamaged Fw190A-3 which was rapidly shipped to RAE Farnborough for detailed examination, after which it went to the Air Fighting Development Unit at Duxford for flight testing.

AFDU pilots confirmed all that had been reported by combat pilots, and in comparison tests with the Spitfire V it was soon evident that the only advantage the British fighter had over the Fw190 was a better turning circle. Aileron control was particularly good and enabled any Fw190 pilot, who found himself bounced by the British fighter, to easily flick into a turn in the opposite direction, which his adversary was hard put to follow. As a result of these tests the AFDU was able to issue certain recommendations to Spitfire pilots, among which was that they should always cruise at high speed. In the event of being attacked, the British fighter should start a shallow dive which would commit the enemy pilot to a tail chase drawing him away from his base, thus limiting combat time when he overhauled the Spitfire which he was almost certain to do. The only asset in direct combat was the Spitfire's turning circle, which could be used to advantage if the Fw190 pilot could be drawn into trying a speed-losing tight turn—it wasn't much comfort, but better than nothing.

More encouraging were the comparisons carried out with the Spitfire Mk IX, which indicated that the supercharged Merlin 61-engined fighter was equal in most respects to the Fw190. The latter had marginally better acceleration and the Spitfire could still not compete with its aileron turns, but at certain altitudes the British aircraft was faster, so the conclusion reached was that below 3,000 feet and between 18,000 to 22,000 feet, the Spitfire IX had the advantage.

The first squadron to be equipped with the Spitfire Mk IX was No. 64 at Hornchurch, which received it in June 1942 and became operational with it in July. On the 30th of the month No. 64 encountered Fw190s for the first time and in a short skirmish with German fighters off the French coast succeeded in shooting down three and damaging two without loss. In a very short space of time the much-in-demand Spitfire was rolling off the production lines and before the famous Dieppe raid in August, four squadrons were equipped with a fighter that was intended only as a stop-gap measure.

The original planned progression had been for the installation of the Merlin 61 in the new Spitfire Mk VIII but the marriage of convenience between the Mk V airframe (later modified) and the two-stage Rolls-Royce engine which produced the Mk IX, was so successful that the Mk VIII saw only

16. British and Canadian pilots being briefed at one of the first landing strips to be established in France after the invasion. (IWM)

17. A Coles Crane of a Canadian unit (note maple leaf roundel on mudguard) helps the removal of the propeller of a Spitfire Mk IX on a French landing strip. (IWM)

18. Sgt H. Stillwell unloads mail from a Hurricane which has arrived in France on an air delivery letter service flight from the UK in the hands of Flt Lt W. V. Melbourne, a New Zealander. (IWM)

19. The Seafire Mk II was a comparatively rare sight in France and here, an example is guided to dispersal in conditions that must have made it feel quite at home! (IWM)

limited service, a total of 1,658 being produced as against the Mk IX's total of 5,739.

On 19 August 1942, the Allies mounted a full-scale reconnaissance of the enemy land defences by sending a force of some 6,000 troops to Dieppe under the code name Operation *Jubilee*. Complete air cover was essential, not only to provide close support and an aerial umbrella for the 252 ships involved, but also to lure the Luftwaffe into the air in an attempt to inflict a paralysing defeat. By this time JG 2 and JG 26 were fully equipped with the Fw190, apart from II/JG 2 and II/JG 26 which were flying the latest Bf109G, which was taken on strength in July. Initial reaction from the Luftwaffe was slow, with only 28 Fw190s from 1, 2, and 3/JG 26 being in the air by 08.00 hrs, but by 10.00 hrs, Do217s from KG 2 and Ju88s from KG 77, which were later joined by He111s of KG 53, were attempting to penetrate the fighter umbrella to attack the mass of ships and landing craft. The efforts of the *Kampfgeschwader* were supported by the fighter-bomber *Staffeln* 10 (*Jabo*) JG 2 and 10 (*Jabo*) JG 26, flying their recently-acquired Fw190A-3/U1 and A-4/U1 aircraft. As withdrawal from the beaches was taking place, the RAF fighter squadrons were fully engaged in providing air cover as well as supporting low-level attacks by Hurricanes, Bostons and Blenheims, which time and again went into support the ground forces. Although by midday many RAF pilots were flying their third and fourth sorties, sometimes meeting fresh enemy pilots flying their first, air superiority had been established in what had become the biggest air battle of the war to date. In the final reckoning, the RAF lost 106 aircraft in 2,617 sorties, of which 88 were Spitfires, whilst the Luftwaffe admitted to losses of 48 against the allied claim of 170.

JG 2 and JG 26 claimed 44 of the RAF aircraft lost, among which was the 50th victory of *Oberleutnant* Egon Mayer; on the debit side they lost 12 Fw190s and two Bf109G-1s. But by the end of the day, II/JG 26 was in for a bigger surprise when B-17E Fortresses bombed its base at Abbeville-Drucat, damaging several aircraft. Two days before Dieppe, the USAAF had opened its daylight bombing campaign with an attack by eleven Fortresses from the 340th, 342nd and 414th Bomb Squadrons of the 97th Bombardment Group, against marshalling yards in the Rouen area. The Fortresses were escorted by four squadrons of Spitfires in what amounted to a short range *Circus* aimed at giving the American crews a taste of action. It was the first of many that were to become commonplace until the full long-range daylight programme planned by the USAAF was instituted. The tight defensive formations of the Fortresses, plus the fighter escort, presented the Fw190 pilots with a formidable problem until they found the answer in new interception tactics which included meeting the American bombers in fast, head-on attacks. The limited range of the Spitfire escorts confined early targets to a radius of some 300 miles, which led to a false sense of security and an under-estimation of the Luftwaffe's capability.

Low-level attacks by bombers and fighter-bombers were not, of course, the sole prerogative of the RAF and Fighter Command still had to maintain à defensive element against similar operations mounted by the Luftwaffe. Coming in low under the radar screen, Bf109s and Fw190s, varying from single aircraft to groups of up to twelve, mounted their own *Rhubarbs* against coastal towns, shipping and military targets. In many cases the damage they caused was not great, but the element of surprise and the wide dispersion of their targets forced the defenders to keep in readiness a defensive arm that was out of all proportion to the numbers of its adversaries. Quite often the raiders had arrived, deposited their bombs and were turning for home before the defending Spitfires were in any position to intercept. A typical example of this occurred on 31 October 1942 when Fw190s of a *Jabostaffel* made a surprise attack on Canterbury. Spitfire Vbs of No. 91 Squadron were scrambled from Hawkinge to intercept the fighter bombers which they succeeded in doing as the Germans made a low-level exit over the Channel. With the advantage of height, the Spitfires dived on the escaping Fw190s and despatched four of them to watery graves, two falling to the guns of South African ace Johannes 'Chris' LeRoux. But by this time the damage had been done and although four enemy aircraft had

20. AC R. Hill of Nottingham, an engine fitter on Auster AOP aircraft, grabs a snack of sardines near the front line in Normandy. He wears the Army XXX Corps shoulder patch, denoting the ground unit to which his observation squadron was attached. (IWM)

been destroyed, it was of little comfort to those who had suffered from their earlier attention. The answer was to mount standing patrols with aircraft capable of catching the low-level raiders on their run-ins. The Typhoon proved to be such an aircraft.

21. Wg Cdr A. G. Page starts a sortie in his Spitfire Mk IXe laden with two 250lb bombs on the wing racks and a 500lb missile on the centreline. The aircraft, which has wheel hub covers in place, shows the pilot's initials painted under the spinner and a rank pennant below the windscreen. (IWM)

22. **An RAF salvage team recovering a damaged Spitfire Mk IX of No. 403 (Canadian) Sqn in France shortly after D-Day. The pilot's seat has been removed, both cannon fairings are missing and the laminated wood propeller blades have severed in what was probably a belly landing. Note lower nose fairing hinged downwards and the jack supporting the centre-section. (IWM)**

ENTER THE TYPHOON

The seven-ton Hawker fighter came from the drawing board of Sidney Camm, who began its design just after his Hurricane had entered RAF service. The Typhoon was destined to have a chequered service career, principally because it was pressed into use before all the development snags with the airframe and engine had been solved. But the need for a fast, heavily armed fighter in 1941 moved the Air Ministry to continually press for its rapid introduction to service and Nos. 56 and 609 Squadrons started to receive Typhoons in November 1941. To both units fell the task of discovering its many faults. It is perhaps reasonable to suggest that if this step had not been taken, the Typhoon story might well have turned out differently, with the aircraft never reaching the service status it eventually achieved. As it was, the decision to introduce the fighter before it was fully developed was justified by the end result, but the price paid in lives during the early stages was high.

During its first nine months of service the Typhoon caused endless problems, which had the effect of a decline in morale of squadrons operating it. From its introduction in November 1941 until September 1942, more Typhoons and their pilots were lost to engine and structural failures than in combat with the Luftwaffe. During standing patrols over the Channel, Typhoons operated at cruising speed below radar surveillance height, so when engine trouble did occur, it gave the pilot little opportunity to bale out; ditching the aircraft, even on the calmest sea, proved difficult because of its large chin-scoop radiator. This feature also presented problems as far as aircraft recognition was

concerned, since from certain angles the new fighter looked very much like the Fw190, and ground gunners were not prone to asking too many questions before opening fire. In an endeavour to help distinguish the types, Typhoon squadrons painted black and white identity bands beneath the wings of their aircraft as well as painting the noses white. This helped to a degree, but in its first month of Typhoon patrols, No. 609 Squadron lost two officers and one sergeant pilot due to mis-identification. More alarming than engine failure or faulty recognition—both of which gave the pilot at least some chance of survival—was the Typhoon's habit of shedding its tail unit. During power dives this section could become detached from the rest of the airframe with only one possible result. During the Dieppe raid, which was the first time the Typhoon was officially mentioned, a section boun-

23. General Eisenhower shows a keen interest in the rocket projectiles fitted under the wings of this Typhoon during a tour of inspection soon after the Hawker fighter arrived in France. (IWM)

ced some Fw190s but two of their number failed to pull out of their intercepting dives due to structural failure. However, it was not all misfortune for the Typhoon, and its superior performance against low-level raiders did achieve enough success for it to be vindicated. Roland Beamont, who had flown in the Typhoon test programme during a rest from operations, and became the CO of No. 609 Squadron in October 1942, was instrumental in championing the new fighter. At a Fighter Command meeting in late 1942, he openly stated that in his opinion it was superior to the Spitfire. At this meeting the whole future of the aircraft was in some doubt, but Beamont's logically argued case won the day with

17

24. **Pilots of No. 66 Sqn just returned from a sweep over Evreux in which they shot down two Fw190s and damaged four more. From the left they are: Flt Lt J. Jackson, W/Off V. Lommen, Fg Off B. Casburn, Fg Off J. Waterhouse and Fg Off A. Brown. (IWM)**

the result that the Typhoon was reprieved and went on to become a first-rate weapon.

During the summer months, No. 1 Squadron was also converting to the Typhoon at Acklington where it had exchanged ageing Hurricanes for the new Hawker fighter in July. This squadron encountered fewer problems than most with the change-over to the big fighter, the only fatal accidents occurring on 21 October, when Plt Off P. Dobie and Gloster Aircraft Company's chief test pilot, Gerry Sayer, failed to return from an air-to-ground firing sortie. No trace was ever found of the two men, who, it is believed, collided over the sea. In the meantime, No. 1 Squadron achieved its first success with the aircraft when Plt Offs Perrin and

Bridges of B Flight were scrambled on 6 September to investigate a hostile radar plot. The two Typhoons climbed to 30,000 feet and quickly identified two Me210s approaching the Tyne. Diving to attack, the Typhoons overhauled the enemy aircraft, which tried to escape by splitting their formation. Plt Off Bridges caught up with his target near Whitby and despatched it into Robin Hood's Bay, whilst Perrin chased his victim south and set it on fire with his cannon before blacking out as he pulled from his dive. Both Me210s were destroyed, bringing the squadron's tally since the outbreak of war to 230, making it the highest scoring RAF fighter unit at that time.

Although defensive patrols continued along the Channel coast, November 1942 saw the Typhoon make its debut in *Rhubarbs*, where its heavy armament made it an ideal foil in the hands of determined pilots. Once again Sqn Ldr Beamont was the man behind the use of the Typhoon in this type of operation, receiving permission from the AOC of No. 11 Group to attack enemy shipping and ground targets with his squadron whenever he could, but at the same time not neglecting the defensive role. On 17 November 1942, No. 609 Squadron carried out its first daytime *Rhubarb* but of more significance was Beamont's solo operation the following night when he attacked railway traffic in the Somme area.

Since the tentative efforts of the day fighter squadrons to intercept enemy bombers in the night blitz of 1940, little serious thought had been given to flying aircraft designed for daylight interception work at night. To operate a still somewhat suspect aircraft on low-level night sorties of the *Rhubarb* type required a high degree of courage. Such was the success of Beamont's first effort, however, that it was not long before everyone wanted to have a go, and soon aircraft operating in pairs by day and usually alone at night, began causing widespread destruction, especially of German rail traffic. Locomotive 'busting' became a profitable part-time occupation for No. 609, the technique being to hit the locomotive first, then knock out the accompanying flak waggon, followed by strafing of the unfortunate occupants. These excursions in no way affected the prime purpose of the Typhoon and on 5 December, F/Sgt Haddon claimed No. 609's first Fw190 after four of these aircraft had attacked the squadron's base. By the middle of March 1943, a further 14 Fw190s had been claimed destroyed during defensive patrols, whilst over 100 locomotives, plus a variety of shipping, had fallen victim to the guns of the squadron. From these early beginnings, the Typhoon was to be developed into a superlative ground-attack fighter, using guns, bombs and rockets.

In many ways, 1943 was a period of consolidation; Fighter Command was now fully on the offensive whilst the Luftwaffe confined itself to sporadic ventures with fighter-bombers and abortive attempts to renew the night blitz. Day fighter squadrons involved on home defence work became more and more envious of their colleagues, who were now almost daily penetrating far into enemy air space, either escorting bombers or seeking their own targets of opportunity.

25. Home Sweet Home. The airmens' mess in an abandoned farmhouse situated near an RAF ammunition dump in France, June 1944. (IWM)

26. LAC George Langley tests the radio telephone of a No. 122 Sqn Mustang III. The hurriedly applied AEAF stripes and red-doped machine-gun port patches are of interest. (IWM)

27. Well-armed RAF Servicing Commandoes relax with a game of cards while a Mustang Mk III of No. 122 Sqn is bombed-up for a ground attack sortie. The rifles and Bren indicate a *very* forward landing ground. (IWM)

In January JG 26 despatched 1 and 7 *Staffeln* to the Eastern Front, which, coupled with the removal of four *Staffeln* of JG 2 to the Mediterranean the previous November, seriously depleted the Luftwaffe force left in Northern France. Although reduced to some 210 serviceable Bf109G-4s and Fw190A-4s with which to meet the growing attentions from the 8th Air Force, 2 Group Bomber Command, and the machines of Fighter Command, the Luftwaffe units which comprised *Luftflotte* 3 still had much to offer in terms of quality. The shortcomings of the training programme had not yet adversely affected them, so JG 2 and JG 26 could still boast a strong nucleus of experienced pilots. Led by *Obstlt* Walter Oesau, JG 2 *Richthofen* was deployed to the west of the Seine whilst JG 26 'Schlageter' under the more flamboyant *Major* Joseph Priller, was located in the Lille area. Unlike Oesau, who commanded his *Geschwader* from an HQ at Beaumont-Le-Roger, Priller flew regularly with his unit and by May 1943 had a personal tally of 87 victories to his credit. In contrast to the RAF, the Luftwaffe did not grant regular rest periods, apart from four week's annual leave, and pilots flew with their units continually—in many cases until they were killed or badly wounded. This is why pilots such as Priller were able to accumulate such

impressive victories. His *Geschwader*, and in particular II *Gruppe* JG 26, now commanded by Adolf Galland's brother, *Hauptmann* Wilhelm-Ferdinand Galland, had frequently tangled with the Biggin Hill Wing. Among JG 26's victims was Sqn Ldr Hugo Armstrong, the CO of No. 611 Squadron, Cmdt J. Schloesing, CO of No. 340 Squadron (shot down in February) and Wg Cdrs R. Milne and J. Slater, lost in March. So, when Wg Cdr J. E. Johnson took command of the Kenley Wing and Wg Cdr A. Deere did likewise for the Biggin Hill Wing, there were plenty of old scores to settle.

Deere's new command gave him the chance to implement his own theories for making the wing system more flexible, which included giving the squadrons more freedom to use their initiative and independence. His daring approach was illustrated on one of his first operations as wing leader when, on the evening of 17 April, he led Nos. 341 and 611 Squadrons to attack I/JG 2's base at Triqueville as the *Gruppe* took off to intercept a raid on Caen. On this occasion, Fw190s had just taken off when Deere's force arrived, and in the ensuing combat, two Spitfires were shot down with nothing to show on the credit side. Success was not long in coming, however and by 15 May the wing's total of enemy aircraft destroyed, which had stood at 983 when Deere took over, had risen to 998. On the afternoon of 15 May the weather was ideal for *Circus* operations and the Biggin Hill Wing was detailed to escort and support Mitchells and Typhoon bombers of No. 181 Squadron attacking Caen-Carpiquet. At the same time, Bostons with escorting Spitfires were detailed to attack the airfield at Poix, where reconnaissance aircraft had reported a large collection of Bf109s.

Fw190s of I/JG 2 bounced the Northolt Wing, which was flying top cover to the Mitchells, and very quickly Gp Capt Pawlikowski and Sgt Lewandowski of No. 314 Squadron were shot down. At this time the Biggin Hill Wing was some way to the south-east of Caen and could not intervene, but its chance came when Fw190s of 2 *Staffel* of I/JG 2 scrambled from Triqueville to help their colleagues over Caen. In the climb to 18,000 feet the *Staffel* became spread out and so anxious was it to catch the

retreating Mitchells, that it failed to notice the Biggin Hill Wing above. Sqn Ldr J. Charles led Yellow Section of No. 611 Squadron into the attack, while Cmdt Mouchotte of No. 341 Squadron turned his section into a 180° diving turn to cut off any Fw190 that avoided Yellow Section's attack. Sqn Ldr Charles caught a pair of Fw190s as they dived towards Caen and saw strikes from his cannon on the rear machine before he overtook it and turned his attention to the leader, who was *Oblt* Horst Hannig, the *Staffelkapitän*. Hannig, who at this time had 90 'kills' to his credit, pulled his aircraft into a turn but Charles's aim was good enough and the Fw190 took the full blast from the Spitfire's guns. One of its wings came off and it cartwheeled to earth. Charles's wingman saw the first Fw190 pilot bale out, so in the space of a few seconds, the Biggin Hill Wing's tally passed the 1,000 mark. Credit for destroying the 1,000th aircraft was shared by Charles and Cmdt Mouchotte, who had shot down a third Fw190 at about the same time.

For the rest of 1943 Fighter Command was involved in a continuation of the work it had started in late 1940 and early 1941, the difference being that more and more aircraft, both bombers and fighters, were now available to the allies and penetration of German airspace became more ambitious. As the

28. Tempest Mk V of No. 3 Sqn at Newchurch shortly after D-Day with AEAF stripes painted over the serial digits. Soon after the squadron moved to Venlo in Holland, the stripes were removed and No. 3's unit emblem was applied to the fin. (IWM)

year wore on, Bomber Command and the 8th Air Force softened-up enemy resistance ready for the invasion which, by the Autumn of 1943, was in the planning stages. As the bombers penetrated deeper they lost their fighter escort, but by the time they had bombed and turned for home, fighters were again airborne ready to pick them up and shepherd them safely to their bases. Defensive patrols over England slackened off as the German fighters were forced into bitter action over the continent where they still represented a force not to be underestimated. But replacement aircraft and well trained crews were now available in greater numbers to the RAF than they were to the Luftwaffe, which could not stand as high a rate of attrition. Since the dark days of 1940 the wheel had turned nearly a full circle, and as squadrons manned by Australians, Canadians, Frenchmen, Poles, Czechs, Americans and many other Western Alliance countries joined the assault, the noose began to tighten. But victory was still 17 months away and the Luftwaffe was by no means a defeated force.

29. Ground crew help a Typhoon pilot into his aircraft. The man standing in front of the starboard wheel holds a fire extinguisher and keeps a wary eye on the mighty Sabre engine. (IWM)

NIGHT OPERATIONS

The advent of the Beaufighter in the night skies of Britain during 1941 and early 1942 heralded the beginning of the end as far as Luftwaffe bomber crews were concerned. Although the ground defences, single-seat fighters and Defiants equipped with early airborne radar, had all taken a toll of the invading bombers, the loss rate was nothing startling and well within the terms of acceptability. But the new twin-engined fighters with heavy armament, improved radar operated by specialist navigators, and a continually improving ground-control system, saw losses begin to escalate.

By April 1942, the Beaufighter was joined by another night fighter which was to become even more feared by the German bomber crews, the De

Havilland Mosquito. It had entered service with No. 157 Squadron in January and the first three months of 1942 were spent readying the new aircraft for operations and ironing out problems encountered with the exhaust systems and flash from the .303 Browning machine guns. As No. 157 worked up it was joined by No. 151 Squadron, which also converted to the type from Defiants.

The 'Baedeker' raids, authorized by Hitler in retaliation for the increasing attention the Fatherland was receiving from Bomber Command, increased the chances of the new fighter making its first kill and rivalry between the two squadrons to record this landmark was intense. The German raids were mounted by small forces of bombers and were aimed at centres of civilian population ranging from Norwich to Exeter, and Birmingham to Hull. On 27 April Norwich was attacked by 47 bombers, and Mosquitoes made several contacts without success. But two nights later 75 bombers returned to East Anglia and Sqn Ldr Ashfield of No. 157 Squadron made contact with a Dornier 217. Ashfield's navigator guided his pilot into an attacking position and visual contact was made. Just as the Mosquito pilot opened fire, an alert member of the Dornier's crew saw it, and the bomber took immediate evasive action. Ashfield's fire appeared to hit the enemy aircraft as it rolled into a dive, but although the night was clear and moonlit, contact was lost and the Dornier was not seen to crash, so only a probable could be claimed. This success served as a spur to No. 151 Squadron, which realized it still had a chance to beat its rivals. That chance came the next evening when Flt Lt Pennington flew the squadron's first Mosquito patrol during further attacks on East Anglia. But he, like his colleagues, was unlucky and although some bombers were shot down, they all fell to Beaufighters.

During these early interceptions, crews had to be extremely careful, as on some occasions their targets turned out to be RAF bombers, so positive identification was an essential before the gun-button was pressed. Otherwise, the disastrous days of 1940–41, when friendly aircraft were shot down because of poor recognition, would have been repeated. Collision was another factor which had to be

30. The RAF's ability to improvise is shown by these pilots, who are using a farm roller weighted with two 500lb bomb casings to help flatten a temporary landing ground in Normandy. Spitfire IXs of No. 602 Sqn can be seen in the background. (IWM)

considered, for at the speed the Mosquito was capable of operating at, it did not take long for a trace on a radar scope to materialize into a lumbering bomber only a few hundred yards away. Speed, however, was essential, for once a German pilot had dropped his bombs, he usually headed home in a shallow dive, gradually building up his speed to some 300 mph. Even a differential of 60 mph could mean a long tail chase for the night fighter crew before they could catch up.

During the evening of 29 May, the Luftwaffe turned its attention to Grimsby and Flt Lt Pennington of No. 151 Squadron intercepted a bomber as it returned over the North Sea. During the succeeding chase, several hits were recorded but the bomber's gunners also managed to damage the Mosquito, which returned on one engine. The following night it was again the turn of No. 157's tenacious Sqn Ldr Ashfield, who caught a Do217

near Dover. He attacked with cannon and machine-gun fire but was again thwarted and could only claim a probable, even though his quarry was seen to dive vertically into cloud. Although it now seems likely that Ashfield's victim did in fact crash, the rivalry between the two squadrons ended in favour of No. 151, whose Wg Cdr I. S. Smith ended the deadlock on the night of 24 June by shooting down two Do217s, one from KG 40 and the other from KG 2, in thirty minutes of intense activity. During June, a No. 157 Squadron pilot located a target on his radar and when visual contact was made he was surprised to find that his quarry was a Bf109F, which evaded the Mosquito and escaped into the

31. The sheer size of the Typhoon can be gauged by this No. 609 Sqn aircraft and its pilot, who is wearing his life-jacket over a No. 1 tunic and has thick white socks rolled down over the top of his flying boots. The machine in the background is MM131. (Via R. L. Ward)

darkness. It was therefore confirmed that the Luftwaffe was now using fighters armed with bombs at night as well as daylight for hit-and-run raids.

During July, enemy activity increased and Mosquitoes claimed six victims, one of which fell to the guns of Sqn Ldr Cooke's aircraft, thus recording No. 264 Squadron's first kill with Mosquitoes, with which it had re-equipped at Colerne in May. The elusive first Mosquito kill for No. 157 Squadron came on 22 August, when the CO, Wg Cdr G. Slade, accounted for a Do217 of KG 2. By the end of the year, four squadrons, Nos. 151, 157, 264 and 85, were operating the Mosquito in the night fighter role, and success was mounting. On some occasions, such as that on 30 September, when a pilot of No. 157 Squadron shot down a Ju88 over the North Sea, the night fighter units were called into operation during the day. This could happen at any time, but was more often than not when the weather was bad, the more experienced instrument flying of the night fighter pilots giving them the edge over their day fighter colleagues. It would be quite correct to claim that this early use of the night fighter during inclement weather was the debut of the post war all-weather fighter.

In January 1943, the Luftwaffe mounted some of its biggest raids since the previous year's attacks on Birmingham, the targets being in the south-east and London. It was during one of these attacks, on 17 January, that Wg Cdr C. Wight-Boycott, the CO of No. 29 Squadron, achieved the distinction of destroying four enemy aircraft in one evening. Flying a Beaufighter, Wight-Boycott first intercepted a Do217 over Folkestone and despatched it to a watery end in the Channel, and then shot down two more of the same type over Kent. To round off a successful evening's work he intercepted a Ju88 over Surrey and saw the crew of four bale out during his attack.

The night fighter squadrons also took part in intruder missions over France, starting with a successful sweep of the Pas de Calais area by Beaufighters of No. 29 Squadron during April. The following month, the squadron recorded its 50th victory at night when Plt Off Crone shot down a He111 as it made its approach into Longvic airfield. This success was achieved, appropriately enough, in the redoubtable Beaufighter, which at this time, was just being replaced on No. 29 Squadron by the Mosquito XII which was a greatly improved version of the Mk II, especially as far as the AI radar was concerned. During May, No. 85 Squadron, now commanded by Wg Cdr J. Cunningham—who had achieved the Beaufighter's first night victory—moved to West Malling and, three days after its arrival added £5 to the beer fund. By this time the Luftwaffe bombers had been taking such a mauling that reprisal raids were being undertaken by fast low-flying fighter bombers, mainly Fw190s. On the night of 16 May, 11 Group scrambled a squadron of Typhoons to combat such a raid as it was considered that the Mosquitoes would be unable to catch the nimble German fighter. Just before midnight it became obvious that the Typhoons were having little success, so the 11 Group Controller took his career in his hands and ordered No. 85's Mosquitoes into the air. First off was Sqn Ldr Green, who was placed by the ground control station at 10,000 feet over the Channel to await further instructions from the fighter controller. Eventually a plot was recorded and Green climbed his aircraft to 18,000 feet where his radar operator, F/Sgt Grimstone, made contact on his AI equipment. Grimstone guided his pilot to a position dead astern of the hostile plot and, as they closed, Sqn Ldr Green identified it as an Fw190 with long-range tanks beneath its wings and a bomb on the fuselage rack. Closing to 100 yards, the Mosquito pilot opened fire with his cannon and after a short burst the enemy aircraft blew up in spectacular fashion, showering the Mosquito with debris. This was one of 17 Fw190s which had raided the south coast that evening and No. 85 Squadron accounted for four of them. Sqn Ldr Green's victim was the first to be destroyed over England, the first Fw190 credited to a Mosquito having gone to Flt Lt Tappin of No. 157 Squadron over France two nights earlier. The victory brought Green a bottle of gin from Wg Cdr Cunningham, a bottle of Champagne from Sqn Ldr Crew and a silver Mosquito model for No. 85's silver collection, as well as the already mentioned £5.

Sporadic raids continued over England, but by this time the defence forces were on top line and although the Luftwaffe used a variety of tactics and aircraft, ranging from Fw190s and Bf109s to Ju88s and the new Me410s, comparatively little material damage was achieved. But these raids did keep a sizeable portion of Fighter Command tied up so, from a strategic point of view, they did a good job as far as the Germans were concerned.

Success with the Mosquito had thus far eluded Wg Cdr Cunningham, who took over No. 85 Squadron in January 1943. The Beaufighter ace and his radar operator, Fg Off 'Jimmy' Rawnsley, had done a great deal in perfecting the use of airborne radar in night fighters and had 16 victories to their credit, but by June they had still to open their account in the Mosquito. On the night of 13 June their fortunes changed. Airborne over the Channel on a standing patrol, they were warned of an approaching raider, onto which the ground controller quickly vectored them. Rawnsley soon found the plot on his screen and guided his pilot into position. The Fw190 was travelling at very high speed but taking no form of evasive action, its pilot presumably believing that his speed would be enough to guarantee safety. The Mosquito commenced a long tail chase, catching the enemy

New Zealand officer fighter pilot, NW Europe, 1944–45. RAF battledress worn with late-model flying helmet and Mae West life-jacket, and 'escape' boots. These had feet like conventional civilian shoes, and a pilot shot down behind enemy lines could convert them by slitting off the suede legs. Laces often concealed wire saw-blades. For low-level operations over enemy lines, service revolvers were often carried in web pistol-belts, either RAF blue or khaki. A pale blue on dark blue 'NEW ZEALAND' flash is worn at the top of each sleeve, and ranking is worn on the blouse shoulder-straps in the form of pale blue on dark blue slip-over tabs.

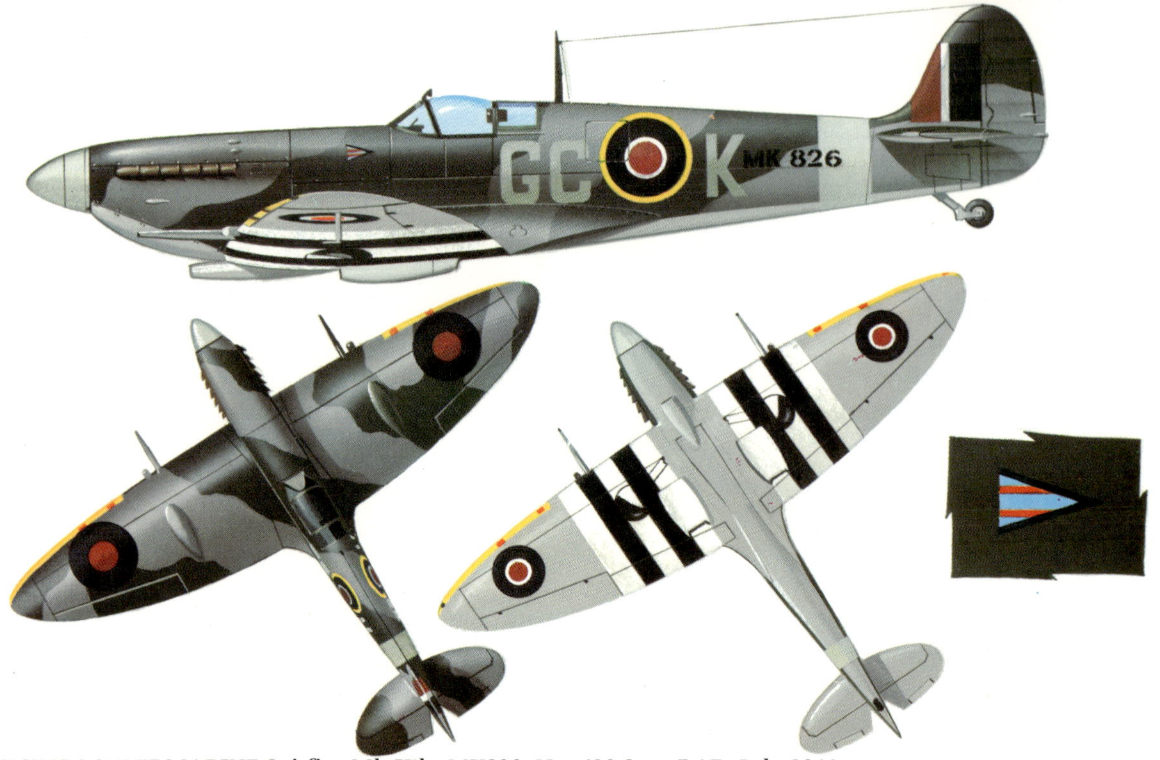

VICKERS SUPERMARINE Spitfire Mk IXb, MK826, No. 412 Sqn. RAF, July 1944

HAWKER Tempest Mk V, NV706, of No. 486 (New Zealand) Sqn. RAF, early 1945

BRISTOL Beaufighter Mk IF, V8324, of No. 29 Sqn. RAF, autumn 1942

OPPOSITE, TOP: Vickers Supermarine Spitfire Mk IXb, MK826, flown by Wing Commander George Keefer from No. 412 Squadron's base at Beny-sur-Mer, Douvres, France in July 1944. The code letters of No. 412 Sqn were VZ, but this machine carries the wing commander's initials. Standard day fighter scheme for the period, with Dark Green and Ocean Grey shadow-shading on upper surfaces and Medium Sea Grey under surfaces. Spinner and rear fuselage band are in Sky, and 18in black and white invasion bands are carried beneath the wings. Roundels are 50in diameter Type B (upper wings), 32in Type C (lower wings) and 36in Type C1 (fuselage); the 24in square fin flash has 11in red and blue stripes and a 2in white stripe. The wing commander's rank pennant pointed rear on port side, forward on starboard side; starboard side codes were painted GC-K. Type B wing with two 20mm cannon and four ·303 machine guns.

OPPOSITE, BOTTOM: Hawker Tempest Mk V, NV706 of No. 486 (New Zealand) Squadron, flying from Volkel, Holland, early 1945. Standard day fighter scheme as Spitfire above.

White spinner, and white individual letter 'F' on both sides of nose. The codes SA-F are in 24in Sky characters; the serial is in regulation 8in black characters. The 18in black and white invasion stripes are marked completely around the wings and the fuselage. Note 50in diameter Type C roundel, replacing Type B on upper wing surfaces from 3 January 1945 onwards. The detail shows the two V-1 flying bomb 'victory' tallies below the cockpit on the port side only.

ABOVE: Bristol Beaufighter Mk IF, V8324, flown by Squadron Leader Richards and Sergeant Mills of No. 29 Squadron from West Malling, Kent, in 1942. Night black overall paint scheme, except dull bronze cowling rings. The 'Bambi and Thumper' motif was painted on the port side only, beneath the windscreen. No roundels were carried on the lower wing surfaces. Note repair patches in lighter shade of black on rudder. This machine made its operational debut on 27 July 1942, and was damaged on 13 November; after repair it passed to No. 51 OTU.

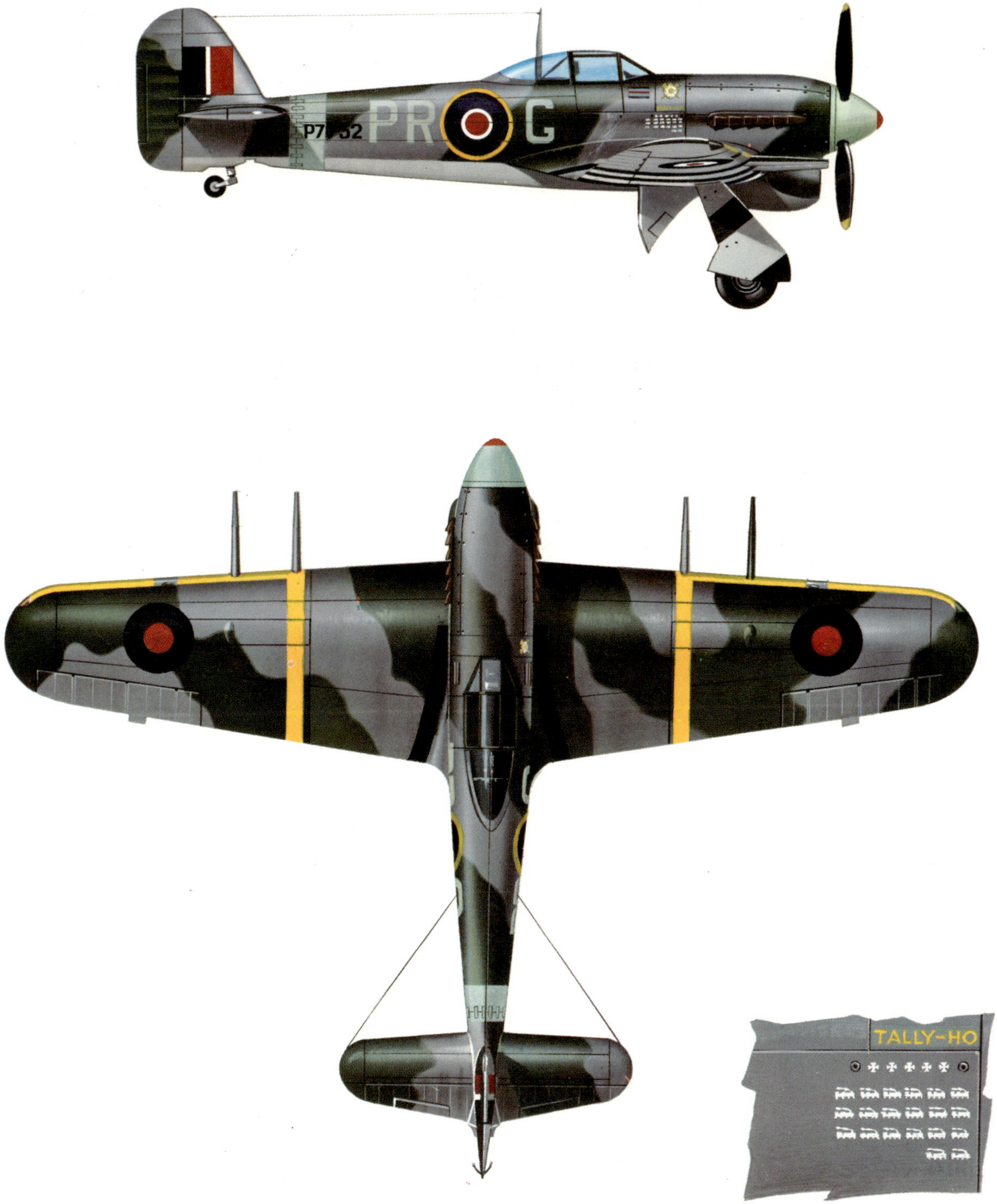

HAWKER Typhoon Mk Ib, P7752, of No. 609 Sqn. RAF, winter 1942–43

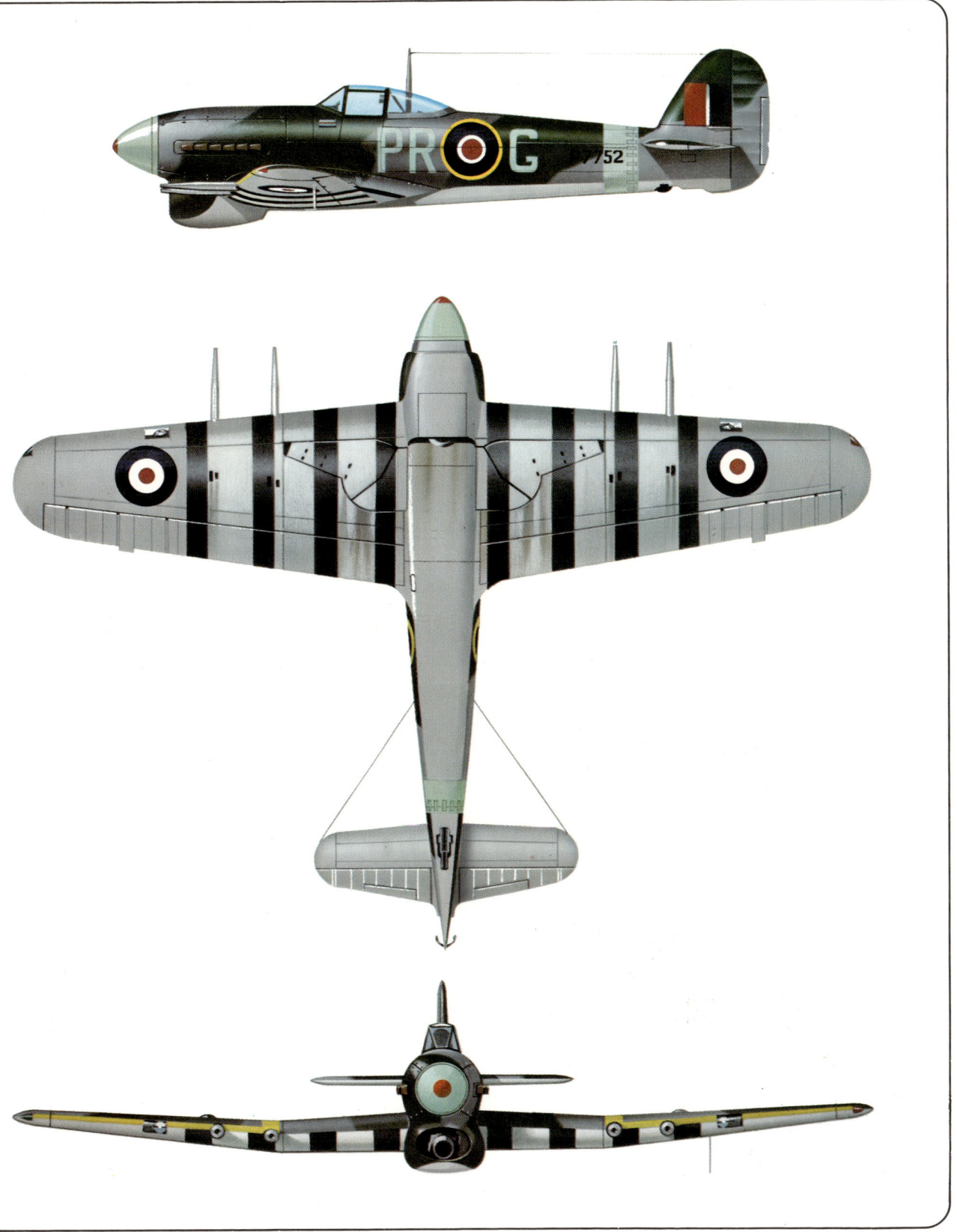

PAGES 28–29: Hawker Typhoon Mk Ib, P7752, flown by Squadron Leader R. P. Beamont of No. 609 Squadron, Auxiliary Air Force, from Manston, Kent, between November 1942 and July 1943. The standard day fighter temperate zone camouflage scheme is carried, in Dark Green, Ocean Grey and Medium Sea Grey (under surfaces). The 18in rear fuselage band and the codes PR-G are in Sky, as is the spinner, which has a red tip. Roundels are 42in diameter Type A1 modified to C1 (fuselage), 42in Type B (upper wings) and 42in Type A (lower wings). The non-standard 24in by 27in fin flash has 11in red and blue and 2in white stripes. The Typhoon carried black and white identification stripes (*not* invasion stripes) beneath the wings, 12in and 18in wide respectively, and a yellow 12in chordwise stripe on the upper wing surfaces.

BELOW: North American Mustang Mk III, FB353, of No. 315 (Polish) Squadron, flying from Peterhead, Aberdeen, Scotland, in November 1944. The camouflage scheme is modified pattern E in Dark Green, Ocean Grey and Medium Sea Grey; codes and fuselage band are in Sky, and the spinner and a 12in nose band are white. Roundels are 40in diameter Type B (upper wings), 40in diameter Type A (lower wings) and 36in Type C1 (fuselage). The Polish insignia was painted on both sides of the nose below the exhaust stacks; the victory scoreboard appeared on the port side only, and included small silhouettes of seven V-1 flying bombs superimposed on swastikas.

OPPOSITE TOP: Insignia details. (A) Personal markings, Tempest Mk V, EJ743, US-H of No. 56 Sqn, Volkel, Holland, December 1944; pilot, F/Sgt A. M. L. Kennaugh. Port side below windscreen. Standard camouflage, Sky fuselage band, invasion stripes under fuselage only. (B) Personal marking, Typhoon Mk Ib, Fg Off Raymond 'Cheval' Lallement of No. 609 Sqn, Manston, Kent, 1942. (C) Personal marking, Typhoon DN421, EL-C of No. 181 Sqn, Odiham, 1943. Starboard, forward of cockpit; standard camouflage. (D) Personal marking, Spitfire Mk IX, BS244, GW-P of No. 340 Sqn, February 1943; pilot Cmdt J. Schloesing, sqn. CO. Standard camouflage, Sky codes; this aircraft shot down over Le Touquet, 13 February, by Fw190s of II/JG 26. (E) Personal marking, Hurricane Mk IIc, BE215, JX-I, of No. 1 Sqn, May 1942; pilot, Sqn Ldr J. A. F. Maclachlan. Standard camouflage, Sky fuselage band, red codes, black undersurfaces without markings. This insignia, under centre exhaust stack, port side, referred to pilot's left arm lost in combat over Malta; he continued to fly with artificial arm until killed over NW Europe in July 1943, with 17 victories to his name. (F) Personal marking, Mosquito Mk II, DZ706, P-YP, of No. 23 Sqn, intruder operations, late 1942; pilot, Fg Off Rudd.

OPPOSITE, BOTTOM: Coles Crane Mk VII series 7, as used by RAF 1942–45, in delivery scheme; some cranes overpainted khaki after delivery, and some hook cradles painted yellow.

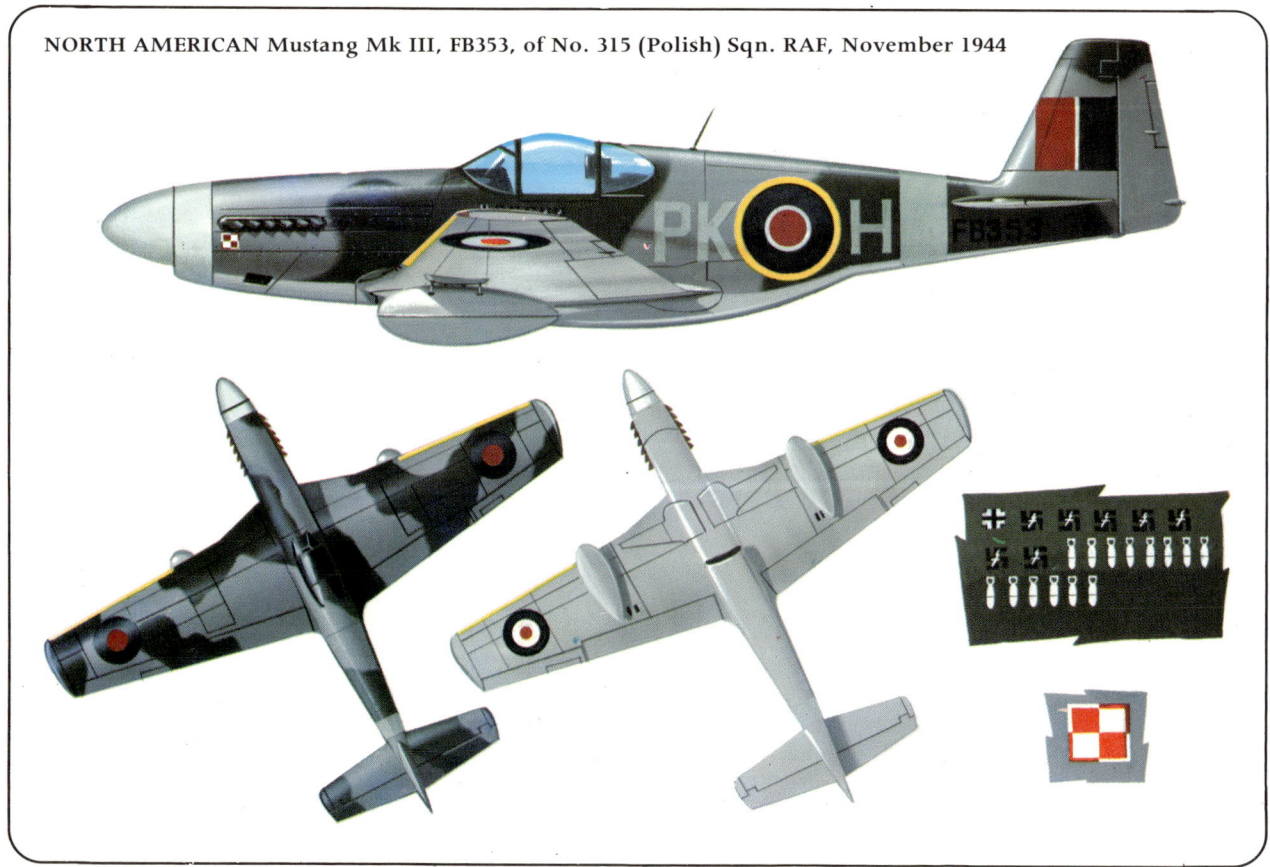

NORTH AMERICAN Mustang Mk III, FB353, of No. 315 (Polish) Sqn. RAF, November 1944

A

B

C

D

E

F

Coles Crane Mk VII series 7

Airman, 2nd Tactical Air Force, Holland, winter 1944. Standard RAF sidecap with brass badge; standard RAF battledress blouse and trousers with Wellingtons and leather jerkin. The albatross badge of all RAF non-commissioned personnel is worn on both shoulders.

Leading Aircraftman, Royal Air Force Regiment, 1943. Formed in February 1942 for airfield defence and associated duties, the regiment wore army battledress with RAF insignia and rank badges. Webbing in RAF blue-grey or khaki was worn. This LAC wears the former, with full 1937 webbing set and a khaki gasmask satchel slung beneath the small pack. He carries the SMLE No. 4 rifle and bayonet, and a grey-painted steel helmet.

32. A rocket-armed Typhoon Mk Ib awaits its turn to torment enemy armour. (IWM)

aircraft in sight of West Malling, where other squadron members left the crew room to see their CO in action. Watchers on the ground heard the roar of the two aircraft, then the thump of cannon fire, followed by the tortured scream of the Fw190's engine as it plummeted earthwards. An explosion, followed by a great ball of fire, marked the end of another enemy aircraft which had been London-bound. It was Cunningham's 17th victory.

The following month the squadron also achieved another notable 'first' when Flt Lt Bunting shot down an Me410 after a fifteen minute chase. The Me410 had been operating in increasing numbers since May and proved a formidable opponent, having a top speed of over 380 mph and rearward defensive armament of two 13mm MG 131 machine guns mounted in remotely controlled barbettes. In addition, it also mounted two 20mm cannon and two 7.9mm machine guns, and could carry a bomb load of 500kg.

In August the Luftwaffe used Me410s to attack Fighter Command airfields, as it had done in 1940, but by now early warning radar was much better and standing patrols of Mosquitoes, Beaufighters and on some occasions, Typhoons, gave little chance of success. But the Luftwaffe was not slow to learn and adopted the tactics used by Fighter Command on its own intruder missions. Me410s were mingled with returning RAF bombers with the object of damaging the runways at their bases, thus forcing them to orbit or divert, whereupon other Me410s would attack. Naturally the bomber crews, tired after a long flight, nursing aircraft which were often damaged or low on fuel, were not given to asking too many questions if a twin-engined fighter appeared near them. So similar were the Mosquito and Me410 that the RAF fighter crews had to be extremely wary when approaching any friendly bomber in case they were mistaken for an enemy intruder by an alert gunner.

Another new German aircraft which made its

33. Loaded with two 1,000lb bombs a Typhoon of No. 439 Sqn sets the spray flying as it starts its take-off run somewhere in France. (IWM)

debut in the skies over England in September was the Ju188 bomber. A greatly improved version of the ubiquitous Ju88, it brought with it an increase in activity by Luftwaffe bomber squadrons. In October, 500 sorties were aimed at London over a period of 21 days but the defences were adequate to parry this new thrust and by the end of the year, the bombers were suffering a loss rate of about 7 per cent. This was not, however, enough to upset the enemy's plans to launch a new night blitz, which came in January 1944, when Ju88s, Dornier 217s, Ju188s—which were only in service with one *Kampfgeschwader*—Me410s and a few of the new He177 bombers, attacked London guided by Fw190s. Only about 6 per cent of the total bomb load, estimated at 500 tons, fell on the capital and this was delivered by approximately 100 of the 500 bombers which had set out on the operation.

Another attempt was made on 29 January to repeat the operation with equally unsuccessful results, even though the ground-control stations' radar was rendered less effective by the use of

Duppel, the German equivalent of RAF Bomber Command's metal foil radar jamming aid 'Window'. Throughout the winter and spring of 1944 the Germans persisted with night raids, the most successful of which came on 18 February, when over 170 tons of bombs were dropped on the capital. But the night fighter squadrons, which were now more active on defence than they had been for a long time, took a terrible toll which forced the Luftwaffe to turn to alternative targets, including Hull, Bristol, Norwich, Portsmouth, Southampton and the centres of population and industry.

After the invasion, during which some night fighter squadrons flew jamming and defensive sorties over the beachheads and France, came the menace of glider and radio controlled bombs, launched by Do217s and He177s and occasionally Ju88s. The same month brought the launching of an even greater menace—the V1.

Intelligence had already warned of the existence of these pilotless ram-jet powered missiles, and both Fighter and Bomber Commands had been engaged in Operation *Noball* attacks on their launching sites; these had succeeded in delaying the Germans, but on 14 June, the offensive began. On the first day, only ten V1s were launched but it was realized that

this was a prelude to the main offensive, which had planned for as many as 500 flying bomb launchings per day. A defensive curtain of guns, balloons and standing patrols of fighters was thrown around London and the south coast and these measures took a tremendous toll of the pilotless missiles.

On 15 June, 244 V1s were launched, of which 73 reached London. Of those destroyed, credit for the first at night by an aircraft went to a No. 605 Squadron Mosquito, flown by Flt Lt Musgrave, who intercepted one over the Channel just after mid-night and shot it into the sea. During the day Spitfires, Tempests and Typhoons took part in anti-*Diver* patrols, as they became known, and at night the Mosquitoes of Nos. 96, 219, 409 and 418 Squadrons assumed the responsibility. The pro-blems of intercepting and destroying V1s were many: the pilotless aircraft travelled at high speed and various altitudes, their small size making them difficult targets, especially when deflection was involved. At night, with only the flame from the missile's engine to home on, the problems were even greater. Shooting from too close a range could result

34. A Spitfire Mk XIV of No. 610 (County of Chester) Sqn Aux.AF on patrol over southern England in late 1943.

in an explosion which could damage or even destroy the attacking aircraft, while firing from too great a range was often ineffective. Most pilots tried to intercept over the sea, since by the time the V1 campaign was at its height, the coastal guns were putting up a solid barrage which was as deadly to friend as it was to foe. Nonetheless, the air defences accounted for a very high proportion of the missiles which continued to be launched until their sites were gradually overrun by the allied advance through Europe.

After D-Day and throughout the rest of 1944 and 1945, nightfighter squadrons were still an essential element of the home defence force, as well as forming an integral part of 2nd TAF on the continent. German raiders continued to make occasional visits to the British Isles and, as late as March 1945, 140 enemy aircraft carried out intruder missions to airfields, shooting down 19 RAF and USAAF bombers. So although activity gradually

35

AIR OFFICERS COMMANDING IN CHIEF, FIGHTER COMMAND 1939–45

Air Marshal Sir Hugh Dowding GCVO, KCB, CMG	July 1936–Nov 1940
Air Marshal Sir W. Sholto Douglas KCB, MC, DFC	Nov 1940–Nov 1942
Air Marshal Sir Trafford Leigh-Mallory CB, DSO	Nov 1942–Nov 1943
Air Marshal Sir Roderic Hill KCB, MC, AFC	Nov 1943–May 1945

2nd Tactical Air Force Order of Battle, 6 June 1944

No. 83 Group
39 (Recce) Wing

Nos. 168, 414 and 430 Squadrons	Odiham	Mustang I
No. 400 Squadron	Odiham	Spitfire XI
121 Wing		
Nos. 174, 175 and 245 Squadrons	Holmesley South	Typhoon Ib
122 Wing		
Nos. 19, 65 and 122 Squadrons	Funtingdon	Mustang III
124 Wing		
Nos. 181, 182 and 247 Squadrons	Hurn	Typhoon Ib
125 Wing		
Nos. 132, 453 and 602 Squadrons	Ford	Spitfire IX
126 Wing		
Nos. 401, 411 and 412 Squadrons	Tangmere	Spitfire IX
127 Wing		
Nos. 403, 416 and 421 Squadrons	Tangmere	Spitfire IX
129 Wing		
No. 184 Squadron	Westhampnett	Typhoon Ib
143 Wing		
Nos. 438, 439 and 440 Squadrons	Hurn	Typhoon Ib
144 Wing		
Nos. 441. 442 and 443 Squadrons	Ford	Spitfire IX

Also attached to this Group were Nos. 653, 658, 659 and 662 Squadrons flying Auster IV AOP aircraft.

No. 84 Group
35 (Recce) Wing

Nos. 2 and 268 Squadrons	Gatwick	Mustang IA
No. 4 Squadron	Gatwick	Spitfire XI
123 Wing		
Nos. 198 and 609 Squadrons	Funtingdon	Typhoon IA
131 Wing		
Nos. 302, 308 and 317 Squadrons	Chailey	Spitfire IX
132 Wing		
Nos. 66, 331 and 332 Squadrons	Bognor	Spitfire IX
133 Wing		
Nos. 129, 306 and 315 Squadrons	Coolham	Mustang III
134 Wing		
Nos. 310, 312 and 313 Squadrons	Appledram	Spitfire IX
135 Wing		
Nos. 222, 349 and 485 Squadrons	Selsey	Spitfire IX
136 Wing		
Nos. 164 and 183 Squadrons	Thorney Island	Typhoon Ib
145 Wing		
Nos. 329, 340 and 341 Squadrons	Merston	Spitfire IX
146 Wing		
Nos. 193, 197, 257 and 266 Squadrons	Needs Oar Point	Typhoon Ib

Also attached to this Group were Nos 652, 660 and 661 Squadrons flying Auster IVs.

No. 85 Group
141 Wing

Nos. 264 and 410 Squadrons	Hartford Bridge	Mosquito XIII
No. 322 Squadron	Hartford Bridge	Spitfire XIV

142 Wing

No. 124 Squadron	Bradwell Bay	Spitfire VII

147 Wing

Nos. 488 and 604 Squadrons	Zeals	Mosquito XIII

148 Wing

Nos. 29 and 409 Squadrons	West Malling	Mosquito XIII
No. 91 Squadron	West Malling	Spitfire XIV

150 Wing

Nos. 3 and 486 Squadrons	Newchurch	Tempest V
No. 56 Squadron	Newchurch	Spitfire IX

AIR DEFENCE OF GREAT BRITAIN

No. 10 Group

No. 1 Squadron	Predannack	Spitfire IX
No. 165 Squadron	Predannack	Spitfire IX
No. 151 Squadron	Predannack	Mosquito XIII
No. 41 Squadron	Bolt Head	Spitfire XII
No. 126 Squadron	Culmhead	Spitfire IX
Nos. 131 and 616 Squadrons	Culmhead	Spitfire VII
No. 610 Squadron	Harrowbeer	Spitfire XIV
No. 263 Squadron	Harrowbeer	Typhoon Ib
No. 68 Squadron	Fairwood Common	Beaufighter VIF
No. 406 Squadron	Winkleigh	Beaufighter VIF

No. 11 Group

Nos. 33, 74 and 127 Squadrons	Lympne	Spitfire IX
Nos. 64, 234 and 611 Squadrons	Deanland	Spitfire Vb
Nos. 80, 229 and 274 Squadrons	Detling	Spitfire IX
Nos. 130, 303 and 402 Squadrons	Horne	Spitfire Vb
No. 345 Squadron *	Shoreham	Spitfire Vb
No. 350 Squadron *	Friston	Spitfire Vb
No. 501 Squadron *	Friston	Spitfire IX
No. 137 Squadron	Manston	Typhoon Ib
No. 605 Squadron	Manston	Mosquito VI
No. 96 Squadron	West Malling	Mosquito XIII
No. 125 Squadron	Hurn	Mosquito XVII
No. 219 Squadron	Bradwell Bay	Mosquito XVII
No. 456 Squadron	Ford	Mosquito XVII
No. 418 Squadron	Holmesley South	Mosquito VI

*These three squadrons were attached to 2nd TAF for the D-Day landings.

No. 12 Group

No. 25 Squadron	Coltishall	Mosquito XVII
No. 316 Squadron	Coltishall	Mustang III
No. 307 Squadron	Church Fenton	Mosquito XII
No. 504 Squadron	Castleton	Spitfire Vb

Detachments of No. 504 Squadron also at Digby and Acklington.

No. 13 Group

No. 118 Squadron	Skeabrae	Spitfire Vb
No. 118 Squadron (Detachment)	Sumburgh	Spitfire Vb
No. 309 Squadron	Peterhead	Hurricane IIc

On 6 June, 1944, Nos. 26 and 63 Squadrons flying Spitfires, 1320 Flight flying Typhoon Ias, and Nos. 808, 885 and 897 Squadrons flying Seafires, all from Lee-on-Solent, were attached to 2nd TAF.

declined over England as it increased over the continent, the fighter pilots based at home could not relax, knowing that they might be called upon at any time to mount either a standing patrol or scramble in pursuit of a hostile intruder. But by this time they also knew that they had superior equipment, better early warning radar, and much greater chance of success and survival than their colleagues had in the dark and distant days of 1940.

THE 2nd TACTICAL AIR FORCE

During the spring of 1943, plans were already being formulated for the invasion of Europe and among them was the provision for a new expeditionary air force to give support to the ground forces. The campaign in North Africa had produced much useful experience in such tactical operations and when the Western Desert Air Force was combined with the North-West African Air Force to form the 1st Tactical Air Force for support of the invasion of southern Europe, similar plans were made to organize a 2nd Tactical Air Force for operations in the west. One of the most successful weapons in the inventory of such a tactical air force was the fighter-bomber, so in preference to expanding the existing, but somewhat dormant Army Co-operation Command, which might have disrupted the non-stop offensive then taking place, it was decided to reorganize Fighter Command.

This was started in June 1943 by the transference of the light bombers of No. 2 Group Bomber Command to Fighter Command, followed soon after by the disbandment of Army Co-operation Command, the squadrons of which were also transferred to Fighter Command. In addition to No. 2 Group, two new groups were set up within the command, each intended for support of one of the armies that would make up the 21st Army Group, the British Commonwealth element of the main invasion force. During the period of reorganization, control of the new air force was still in the hands of Fighter Command, which continued to plan and mount sorties against railways, communication systems and military installations in France and the Low Countries. During this period the Venturas of No. 2 Group suffered disastrous losses and were replaced by Mosquito Mk VI fighter-bombers which continued to support the efforts of existing Mitchell and Boston units in the medium-level bombing role,

35. The Tempest V was the fastest piston-engined fighter to see RAF service during the war. The stripes under the wings of this machine are the special identity markings applied to both Typhoons and Tempests until February 1945. Each white band is 18in wide and the black one is 12in, whereas invasion stripes were three white and two black, each 18in wide. (IWM)

whilst Typhoons and Hurricanes, armed with bombs and occasionally rocket projectiles, looked after the low-level assault missions. The versatile and still formidable Spitfire provided fighter cover for these operations.

On 13 November 1943 Air Chief Marshal Sir Trafford Leigh-Mallory took command of the new Allied Expeditionary Air Force, which comprised the US 9th Air Force, the 2nd Tactical Air Force and the Air Defence of Great Britain squadrons. The latter two elements were formed on 15 November, Fighter Command being dissolved. Air Marshal Arthur Coningham, a previous commander of the Western Desert Air Force, took over the reins of 2nd TAF with Air Vice Marshals Harry Broadhurst and L. Brown as his 83 and 84 Group Commanders, and Air Vice Marshal Basil Embry in charge of No. 2 Group. Leigh-Mallory's place as AOC-in-C Fighter Command, which was now in effect the squadrons remaining in ADGB, was taken by Air Marshal Roderic Hill.

Although the various changes in the chain of command did cause some problems, operations continued in much the same way as they had done for the last two years, with the emphasis on obtaining complete control of enemy airspace whilst creating as much damage to ground installations and troop movements as possible. As the planned invasion drew nearer, a further group, No. 85, was formed, its task defined as the defence of the areas in which invasion equipment was being stockpiled as well as of the 2nd TAF bases. This group was equipped with Mosquito and Beaufighter night fighters plus two squadrons of the new Griffon-engined Mk XIV Spitfires and one of high altitude Mk VII Spitfires.

Training in the use of new armament, including rocket projectiles, and photographic and visual reconnaissance, much of which was assigned to the Mustang, was carried out on a rotation basis as the 2nd TAF squadrons gradually built up their expertise to achieve their two main objectives when the invasion took place. These objectives were: to gain complete air superiority to enable bomber and reconnaissance aircraft to have freedom of operation; and to provide a very high level of air support

36. 'Ger off'. A ground crew fitter tussles with the starboard undercarriage leg of a Typhoon. (Via R. L. Ward)

to the army on the ground, the latter operations being required at any time and in extreme weather conditions.

During April and May, a systematic series of pre-invasion operations were mounted against transport systems, strategic bridges, coastal defences, airfields, and radar installations. As part of this softening-up process, Typhoons of No. 438 Squadron became the first aircraft of this type to use 1,000 lb bombs, when they attacked *Noball* sites and bridges on 24 April. Losses on these low-level sweeps, which were frequently undertaken at wing strength, were high and included some very experienced pilots. But the damage they did, especially to radar sites, paved the way for an easier assault than would have been possible if the enemy had not been denied the ease of communication and early warning so essential to a defending force. There can be no doubt that the losses suffered by the RAF at this time significantly reduced the number of casualties inflicted on the invasion forces, so the overall picture was not as grim as it might have been.

To help the decoy that had been laid in a successful attempt to convince the German High Command that the invasion was to take place in the Calais area, a series of attacks was mounted on radar stations in this area during the five days prior to D-

37. The Tempest Mk V of Wg Cdr Roland Beamont during the time he led the Newchurch Wing. The aircraft carries the pilot's initials in code letter form and a wing commander's pennant appears below the windscreen. (IWM)

Day. These strikes were so effective that all radar stations in the area, except one, were destroyed by the attacking fighter bombers. The one that survived was deliberately spared so that it could pick up false echoes during the night before the invasion, thus completing the deception that the main force was indeed heading towards Calais.

In the week prior to the Allied assault, all aircraft of the AEAF were painted with black and white identity stripes as aircraft recognition had for a long time been a particular weakness of the army and navy gunners! These stripes were applied to wings and fuselages, more often than not in a hurry and with any size of brush that happened to be available.

On 6 June 1944, the initial assault on the Normandy beaches was made by five seaborne and three airborne divisions, whilst the AEAF provided nine squadrons over the beaches on a rotation basis throughout the day. The huge aerial and seaborne armadas which converged on France throughout the day and night were ably protected by Spitfires, P-47s and P-38s, the latter patrolling the Channel to give aerial cover to the ships bringing equipment, supplies and troops. Mustangs, Spitfires, FAA Seafires and a flight of Typhoons carried out armed reconnaissance as well as performing spotting duties for naval guns and artillery once the latter was established ashore.

To combat this huge allied air force, the Luftwaffe could only muster a total of 160 day fighters, most of them from JG 2 and JG 26, plus some 50 night fighters. As a result of the allied air offence in the days prior to the invasion, many of the German fighter units were denied the use of forward airfields, and had been dispersed over a wide area. During the opening phase of Operation *Overlord* much of the initial work fell on the shoulders of JG 2 which had been sadly depleted but was not as badly off as JG 26 which, though numerically strong, had its elements well scattered, I *Gruppe* being at

38. Tempest Mk V, EJ555 of No. 501 (County of Gloucester) Sqn Aux.AF at Hawkinge, in 1945. (Via R. L. Ward)

Rheims, II *Gruppe* on detachment to a base near the Pyrenees, and III *Gruppe* in Alsace. Only two Fw190A-8s of the *Geschwaderstab*, those of *Oberstleutnant* Priller and his wingman, *Unteroffizier* Wodarczyk, remaining in the area of the invasion. Consequently, there was little aerial activity on the opening day, but the Luftwaffe quickly poured reinforcements into the area, and the RAF began encountering enemy aircraft in ever increasing numbers.

On the second day of the operation, more aircraft from AEAF were released for offensive sorties, with Typhoons concentrating on targets in the immediate area and Mustangs using their great range to roam further afield. The American-built fighter has rarely been given the credit it deserves for operations with the RAF in the European Theatre; although over-shadowed by the Spitfire in the interceptor role, it was used extensively for low-level photographic reconnaissance and army support. It could hold its own at low-level with the Bf109 and Fw190 if it had to and in fact on D-Day, Flt Lt Hancock and W/Off Rigby of No. 129 Squadron shot down one of the

few Luftwaffe fighters to be seen on that day, this being an Fw190 which attempted to interfere with one of the airborne forces' glider assaults. The following day came another example of the Mustang's versatility when, during an attack on marshalling yards, 30 Bf109s appeared and were engaged by No. 306 Squadron, which shot down five and damaged three. In the afternoon of the same day, No. 306 again encountered Bf109s during an armed reconnaissance, and this time claimed six victims.

By 10 June, the Luftwaffe fighter force in the area had been strengthened by I, II, and III/JG 1, I and II/JG 11, II and IV/JG 3, I, III, IV and the *Stab* of JG 27 and III/JG 54. The popular belief that the Allies met very little aerial opposition during the invasion is therefore unfounded, except, of course, on the first day. The German fighter pilots began to take a heavy toll of the AEAF, but at the same time suffered badly themselves. Over 400 single-engined

41

39. Shipping at Porsgrunn under attack from Mosquitoes, 11 April 1945.

fighters had been lost by 1 July, as well as 224 bombers in aerial combat and a further 137 aircraft of all types destroyed in strafing operations.

As the Allied advance progressed and landing grounds were set up, initially as emergency strips, then as re-arming and refuelling points, the pressure could be increased. The German fighter units found it more and more difficult to operate as co-ordinated tactical units and had to rely on the initiative of individual *Staffel* commanders, rather than a properly-planned defensive strategy. In addition, fuel became a problem and by mid-June shortages were seriously curtailing air operations. But the Luftwaffe did not lack replacement aircraft for, by this time, the German war machine was producing

more aircraft than it had done at any other time in the war. Increased production did not immediately help the hard pressed *Jagdgeschwadern* in France, but in the long term it did enable the severe losses of the summer to be made good so that by October, all fighter units had been brought back up to strength. Six new fighter units had also been formed to defend the German homeland.

As the allied forces established and then broke out of the beachheads, beginning the advance that was to take them to victory, the German Army began to feel the weight of real air power. Rocket-firing Typhoons, supported by Mitchells and Mustangs, made the ground a distinctly unhealthy place as roads, gun emplacements and assembly points were bombed and strafed. Even well-established military headquarters well behind the front line were heavily attacked. In an attempt to retaliate, the

Luftwaffe was called upon to mount similar operations, but lack of proper aircraft, flown by pilots who were not trained in this type of aerial warfare, proved the exercise to be a costly one. Many of the fighters that were lost on such sorties would have been better employed trying to gain some measure of air superiority, but by then the Spitfires and Tempests which had entered service with Nos. 3 and 56 Squadrons in April controlled the air. Ground-attack aircraft could thus operate in comparative safety, their losses from ground fire being far higher than from enemy fighters.

The Tempest proved to be one of the fastest Allied fighters and, after initial work in the ground attack role prior to D-Day, came into its own against the V1, claiming 638 of the RAF's total of 1,771 destroyed from June to September 1944. With the 2nd TAF, the Tempest distinguished itself during the advance through Belgium and Holland, playing a big part in aerial support for the abortive Arnhem landings, as well as being one of the few aircraft capable of catching the Me262 jet fighter, which began to appear in late 1944. The first of the German jets to fall to a Tempest was credited to Plt Off R. Coles of No. 122 Wing on 8 October over Grave. With the German Army being pushed back into its own country, the 2nd TAF carried out a round-the-clock assault. By day, fighters patrolled the sky at will seeing less and less opposition, whilst at night, Mosquitoes, Mitchells and Typhoons intruded, bombed and intercepted any German bombers that dared to venture over allied-controlled airspace. But in the same way that the RAF defended England in 1940, the Luftwaffe continued to offer spirited resistance, inflicting losses which could now easily be sustained, but served to avoid complacency on the part of Allied Airmen. The hard-pressed German infantry and armour units were under continual attack from Typhoons, Tempests and Mustangs, which by now were operating a system of standing patrols known as 'Cabranks'. Heavily-armed Typhoons would patrol in a given area and could be called into action by local army commanders, whose advance may have come to a temporary halt due to a well-concealed tank or gun emplacement. Direct contact with the leader of the Typhoon section,

40. The Spitfire Mk XIV, RN114, of Wg Cdr R. C. Waddell, wing leader of No. 39 Photo-Reconnaissance Wing, at Eindhoven in January 1945. (Via R. L. Ward)

during which details of map reference and type of target were passed, would bring a concentrated attack by cannon fire and rockets, sometimes only a few hundred yards ahead of the allied force involved. Such co-operation invariably cleared the way in a very short space of time.

On New Year's Day 1945, the Luftwaffe hit back with a surprise low-level raid on several allied airfields, using nearly 900 aircraft. Led by experienced navigators in Ju88s, this huge final fling caught many units of the 2nd TAF unawares and at some airfields, where aircraft had been neatly lined up in rows, the devastation was tremendous. It is estimated that at least 144 British aircraft were destroyed on the ground, and although the Luftwaffe lost over 200 machines, it had reminded the Allies that it was not quite a spent force yet. But lack

41. Spitfire Mk XIVs at Petit Bosel, Belgium in 1945. Nearest the camera is RM820 with RM910/Y behind. (Via R. L. Ward)

of fuel, ammunition, communications and experienced pilots, all combined to bring a once seemingly unbeatable air force to its knees. Luftwaffe units continued to fight in isolation until the final days of the war, one being *General* Adolf Galland's JV 44, which was formed from remnants of units operating Me262s. This nucleus of experienced pilots, flying the German jet, operated from München-Augsberg autobahn until it transferred to a base at Salzburg/Maxglam, where it was finally surrendered on 3 May.

So in the last days of the war the whine of jet engines, first heard in combat from the Me262, then to a lesser degree the Meteors of No. 616 Squadron, which saw action against the V1 and limited use in France, heralded the end of a conflict which had seen air power used to tremendous advantage by both sides. It also saw the dawn of a new type of aircraft which in the following few years would bring speeds hitherto undreamed of by the fighter pilots of the RAF and Luftwaffe and would also carry a deterrent that would make world war a thing of the past.

THE AIRCRAFT

De Havilland Mosquito N.F. Mk XIII
Powerplant Two 1,460hp Rolls-Royce Merlin 23s *Span* 54ft 2 in *Length* 40ft 10¾in *Height* 15ft 3½ins *Weight empty* 14,300lb *Combat weight* 18,100lb *Maximum speed* 356 mph *Cruising speed* 328mph *Climb to 15,000ft* 6·75 mins *Service ceiling* 34,500ft *Range* 1,520 miles *Armament* four 20mm Hispano cannon with 150rpg

Bristol Beaufighter Mk VIF
Powerplant Two 1,670hp Bristol Hercules VI or XVI *Span* 57ft 10in *Length* 41ft 8in *Height* 15ft 10in *Weight empty* 14,600lb *Combat weight* 21,600lb *Maximum speed* 333mph *Cruising speed* 276mph *Service ceiling* 26,500ft *Range* 1,480 miles *Armament* Four 20mm Hispano cannon with 240rpg and six 0·303 Browning machine guns with 1,000rpg

Hawker Typhoon Mk 1b
Powerplant One Napier Sabre 2,200hp IIB or 2,260hp Sabre IIC *Span* 41ft 7in *Length* 31ft 11in *Height* 15ft 3½in *Weight empty* 8,800lb *Combat weight* 13,250lb *Maximum speed* 412mph *Cruising speed* 330mph *Climb to 15,000ft* 5·9mins *Service ceiling* 35,200ft *Range* 510 miles (980 with external fuel) *Armament* four 20mm Hispano cannon with 140rpg plus eight 60lb rockets or up to 2,000lb of bombs

Hawker Tempest MkV
Powerplant One 2,180hp Napier Sabre II *Span* 41ft *Length* 33ft 8in *Height* 16ft 1in *Weight empty* 9,250lbs *Combat weight* 11,500lbs *Maximum speed* 427mph *Cruising speed* 391mph *Climb to 15,000ft* 5mins *Service ceiling* 36,000ft *Range* 740 miles or 1,530 miles with external fuel *Armament* four 20mm Hispano cannon with 150rpg plus eight 60lb rockets or up to 2,000lb of bombs

North American Mustang Mk III
Powerplant One 1,695hp Rolls-Royce Packard Merlin *Span* 37ft *Length* 32ft 3in *Height* 8ft 8in *Weight empty* 6,985lb *Combat weight* 9,800lb *Maximum speed* 426mph *Cruising speed* 397mph *Climb to 15,000ft* 6min. *Service ceiling* 42,000ft *Range* 955 miles *Armanent* Four 0·50 Browning machine guns with 350rpg (inboard pair) 280rpg (outboard pair) plus up to 2,000lb of bombs

Supermarine Spitfire Mk IX (Figures in parentheses for Mk V)
Powerplant One 1,720hp (1,470) Rolls-Royce Merlin 66 (45) *Span* 36ft 10in *Length* 31ft 4in *Height* 12ft 7¼in (11ft 4¾in) *Weight empty* 5,800lb (5,100) *Combat weight* 7,500lb (6,785lb) *Maximum speed* 404mph (374mph) *Cruising speed* 338mph (322mph) *Climb to 20,000ft* 6·4mins (8mins) *Service ceiling* 42,500ft (37,000ft) *Range* 434 miles (470 miles) *Armament* Two 20mm Hispano cannon with 120rpg and two 0·5 Browning machine guns with 250rpg, plus up to 1,000lb of bombs (two Hispano cannon and four 0·303 machine guns)

1 Revue de Mustangs à Andover, 1942. Ces appareils à moteur Allison du début portent des insignes du Guards Armoured Division, auquel fut attaché l'escadron à l'époque. 2 Sqn. Ldr. Maclachlan perdit un bras au combat au-dessus de Malte et peignit un insigne approprié sur son Hurricane Mk IIC, lorsqu'il était attribué à des devoirs d'intrusion au-dessus de l'Europe. 3 Typhoon Mk Ib avec une carlingue type 'porte de voiture' du début et des rayures d'identification en dessous des ailes. 4 Une des quatre unités Spitfire dans un No. 1 Polish Fighter Wing était No 306 Escadron, un Spitfire Mk IX qu'on voit ici. 5 Des pilotes du No. 315 (Polish) Sqn. devant un Mustang III du Capt. Horbaczewski, deuxième sur la gauche. L'avion est décoré avec le tableau impressionnant du pilote. 6 Un No. 306 Sqn. Mustang branché à un chariot démarreur et prêt à faire une sortie 'anti-Diver'. 7 Un pilote Mosquito et navigateur portant un gilet de sauvetage Mae West, masque d'oxygène, casques et foulards de soie pour prévenir contre l'écorchement du cou en cherchant les avions ennemis. 8 Le même équipage Mosquito avec deux styles de bottes de pilote. 9 Spitfire Mk IXc chasseurs du No. 349 (Belgian) Sqn. à Friston, UK. 10 L'arme meutrière du Mosquito FB Mk IV.

11/12 Des buts flottants sous l'attaque des Mosquitos pendant une grève Roastead anti-navigation. 13 Attendant de faire une sortie d'intrusion depuis West Malling, UK, voilà un Mosquito NF XII du No. 29 Sqn. 14 Le premier Spitfire à atterrir en France après le Jour J en train de faire le plein avec des RAF Servicing Commandos, utilisant des bidons d'essence et un entonnoir. 15 Prefabricated Bitumised Strips étant empilés dans un dépôt en France. PBS créa une base ferme pour des bandes perforées en métal transformant des terrains non préparés rapidement en terrains d'aviation. 16 Mise au courant de pilotes de chasse à l'un des premiers terrains d'aviation utilisés en France après l'invasion. 17 Une grue aide les équipages au sol à enlever l'hélice d'un Spitfire Mk IX. 18 Bien qu'il fut un chasseur du front du Jour 'J', le Hurricane servit toujours. Ici le courrier vient d'être livré du Royaume-Uni au terrain d'aviation français. 19 Un Seafire Mk II est conduit à travers la boue à un terrain d'aviation du front ? assez tôt après les atterrissages sur le continent. 20 RAF Aircraftsman Hill portant un écusson de l'Armée à l'épaule indiquant la formation au sol à laquelle son escadron d'observation Auster fut attribué pendant l'époque de l'invasion.

21 Un Spitfires Mk IXe portant des bombes avec les initiales du pilote sous l'hélice et avec le pennon du Wing Commander sous le pare-brise. 22 Avec son hélice en bois contre-plaqué cassé, la gaine du capot basculé et la gaine des canons enlevés, ce Spitfire vient d'être récupéré par une équipe RAF de sauvetage. 23 General Eisenhower faisant l'inspection d'un Typhoon armés de fusée. 24 Quatre pilotes de Spitfire de l'escadron No. 66 après une sortie oùils abattirent deux Fw 190s et abimèrent quatre de plus. 25 Une maison de ferme française utilisée comme Mess par les aviateurs RAF. 26 Un test de radio téléphone pour un Mustang III qui avait des rayures AEAF et des pièces enduites de rouge au-dessus des places des mitrailleuses. 27 Des canons prêts, RAF Servicing Commandos, attendent la prochaine sortie chasseur bombardiers, par les Mustangs du No. 122 Sqn. depuis un terrain d'aviation du front. 28 Les rayures noires et blanches 'invasion' sur les avions alliés devinrent familières aux amis et ennemis pareils. On les voit sur un Tempest V du No. 3 Sqn. 29 Des incendies de moteurs étaient courantes avec le bloc-moteur Typhoon-Napier et lorsqu'on le chauffait, un homme se tenait prés avec un appareil extincteur. 30 Deux 500lb. bombes faisant le poids sur un rouleau de ferme utilisé pour aplâtir un terrain d'aviation RAF improvisé.

31 Un pilote du No. 609 Sqn. donnant l'échelle au Typhoon massif. 32 Le fléau des Panzers. Les Typhoons avec des projectiles fusées se préparent pour une autre sortie. 33 Même dans des conditions telles que celles-ci, la pression des Alliés était maintenue. Un Typhoon roule à travers la boue sur un terrain français. 34 Un moteur Griffon Spitfire Mk XIV en patrouille au-dessus du Sud d'Angleterre, fin 1943. 35 Un Tempest V indiquant les rayures d'identification appliquées aussi bien aux Typhoons qu'aux Tempest afin d'éviter la confusion avec les Fw190. Ces marques différent des rayures AEAF par les bandes noires de 12 inches de largeur. 36 Changeant une roue d'un Typhoon donna parfois des problèmes! 37 Avec les initiales du Wg. Cdr. Roland Beamont, comme lettres de code, ce Tempest V a aussi un pennon de rang sous le pare-brise. 38 Tempest V du No. 501 Sqn. Auxiliary Air Force a Hawkinge, UK, 1945. 39 Des Mosquitoes attaquant la marine à Porsgrunn, avril 1945. 40 Spitfire Mk XIV piloté par Wg. Cdr. Waddell du No. 39 Photo-Reconnaissance Wing, Eindhoven, janvier 1945. 41 Une paire de Spitfire XIVs à Petit Bosel, en Belgique, en 1945.

Notes sur les planches en couleurs

Page 25 : Officier chasseur pilote Nouvel Zélandais en tenue de campagne RAF dernier modèle de casque. Un gilet de sauvetage Mae-West et des bottes de 'fuite' avec les jambes détachables en daim. Des revolveurs étaient souvent portés pendant des opérations à basse altitude au-dessus des lignes ennemies sur des ceintures bleues ou khakis. En haut de chaque manche se trouve l'écusson de nationalité bleu pâle sur bleu foncé, avec des insignes de rangs sur des pattes sur les épaulettes de la chemise en bleu pâle sur du bleu foncé.

Page 26 en haut: Spitfire Mk IXb, MK 826, de l'escadron No. 412 piloté par Wg. Cdr. George Keefer de Beny-sur-Mer, Douvres, France, juillet 1944. Les initiales du pilote portées comme des lettres de codes, remplaçant les unités de code standard, qui étaient 'VZ'. Le dessin de camouflage est courant pour l'époque, vert foncé et gris océan avec des dessous en gris de mer moyen. La bande sur l'hélice et ce fuselage en bleu ciel et les rayures d'invasion 18 inches apparaissent sur les dessous des ailes. Le pennon de rang indique le devant côté, tribord, l'arrière, côte bâbord, les codes côté tribord se lisent GC-K.

Page 26 en bas: Tempest Mk V, NV 706 du No. 486 Sqn., à Volkel, Hollande, début 1945: Combinaison de camouflage comme pour le Spitfire, avec un pennon blanc et une lettre individuelle 'F' sur les deux côtés du cône; les codes du ciel et des rondeaux de série, noirs Type B sur les surfaces supérieures des ailes étaient remplacées par Type C. Vue en détail montre deux symboles de victoires de bombardier sous la carlingue, côté bâbord seulement.

Page 27: Beaufighter Mk IF, V8 324 de l'escadron No. 29, piloté par Sqn. Ldr. Richards, et Sgt. Mills depuis West Malling, Kent, UK, 1942. Couverture de nuit noire, avec insigne Walt Disney, 'Bambi et Thumper', côté bâbord seulement. Des endroits réparés sur le gouvernail ont des tâches en couleur moins foncée.

Page 28–29: Typhoon Mk Ib, P7752 du No. 609 Sqn. Auxiliary Air Force, piloté par Sqn. Ldr. R. P. Beamont, de Manston, Kent, UK, novembre '42–juillet '43. Combinaison de camouflage 'temperate' RAF standard chasseur de jour avec des codes ciel et l'hélice à bout rouge. Les rayres d'identification Typhoon/Tempest sous les ailes avec une rayure jaune sur les surfaces supérieures des ailes. Marques personnelles, côté tribord seulement, se composaient de la rose blanche de York au dessus de deux cors de chasse, surmontées par les mots utilisés couramment 'TALLY HO', qu'en langage RAF voulait dire 'Engagez l'avion ennemi'. Les deux mots étaient jaunes sur fond ciel au dessus du tableau de chasse personnel du pilote. Le pennon de rang apparaissait sur les deux côtés.

Page 30: Mustang Mk III, FB 353, du No. 315 (Polish) Sqn. à Peterhead, Aberdeen, Ecosse, novembre 1944. La combinaison de camouflage est le dessin modifié E en gris océan/gris de mer moyen; les codes en ciel, avec l'hélice et 12 inches du cône devant en blanc, ce dernier étant une marque de reconnaissance de RAF Mustang IIIs. Des rondeaux Type B de l'aile supérieure Type A sous les ailes. Les insignes polonais sur les deux côtés du cône sous les échappements et tableau, côté bâbord seulement. En faisant des patrouilles 'anti-Diver', cet avion détruisit sept V-Is. Depuis le 17 août 1944, les rayures jaunes de

commandement étaient enlevées de l'avion pendant des interceptions de bombardement, mais étaient remises lorsque certains appareils retournèrent à du travail d'escorte.

Page 31: Détails des insignes (A) Des marques personnelles du Flt. Sgt. A. M. L. Kennaugh, Tempest V EJ743, US-H du No. 56 Sqn. (B) Marques personnelles du Flg. Off. R. 'Cheval' Lallament, Typhoon Mk Ib, No. 609 Sqn. (C) Marques personnelles Typhoon DN 421 El-C du 181 Sqn. (D) Marques personnelles du Cmdt. J. Schloesing Spitfire Mk IX, BS 244, GW—P du No. 340 Sqn. (E) Marques personnelles Sqn. Ldr. J. A. F. Maclachlan, Hurricane Mk IIC, BE 215, JX-I, No. 1 Sqn. (F) Marques personnelles Flg. Off. Rudd, Mosquito Mk II DZ 706, P-YP No. 23 Sqn.

Page 31 en bas: Coles Crane Mk VII series 7, utilisé par le RAF 1942–45 en combinaison de couleur de livraison. Certaines grues en service étaient peintes en khaki, certains crochets étant jaunes. Le numéro d'immatriculation était habituellement au centre du pare-choc.

Page 32 à gauche: Leading Aircraftsman, RAF Regiment, 1943. Inauguré en février 1942 pour ces besoins de défense des terrains d'aviation, l'uniforme RAFR était la tenue de campagne de l'Armée avec des insignes de rangs et écusson RAF. Les sangles étaient bleu-gris RAF ou khaki comme indiqué, avec un ensemble de sangles complets d'avant-guerre et un sacoche de masque à gaz.

Page 32 à droite: Airman 2nd Tactical Air Force, en Hollande, hiver 1944. Un calot règlementaire RAF avec un attribut en cuivre, chemise et pantalons tenue de campagne RAF avec des bottes Wellington et un justaucorps en cuir. Un attribut Albatross de tout le personnel RAF sous-officier est porté sur les deux épaules.

ÜBERSCHRIFT

1 Eine Musterung von Mustangs, Andover 1942. Dieser Staffel wurde de Guards Armoured Division zugeteilt, deshalb sind die Abzeichen der Division an den Rumpfen getragen worden. Die Maschinen sind mit Allison Motoren ausgerüstet. 2 Sqn Ldr Maclachlan verlor seinen Arm in einer Luftschlacht über Malta. Als er später Jagdeinsätze über Europa machte, brachte er ein passendes Abzeichen an den Rumpf seiner Hurricane Mk IIC Maschine an. 3 Eine Typhoon Mk Ib mit den Kanzel 'Autotüren' die anfänglich zu sehen waren. Die Erkennungsstreifen an den Flügelunterseiten beachten! 4 Eine Spitfire Mk IX von No. 306 Sqn, einer der vier Spitfire-Einheiten die mit No. 1 Polish Fighter Wing dienten. 5 Piloten von No. 315 (Polish) Sqn vor der Mustang III von Capt. Horbaczewski (2. von links). Die einsdrucksvolle Siegestafel am Flugzeugrumpf beachten! 6 Diese Mustang von No. 306 Sqn steht startbereit, mit dem Batteriefahrzeug gekoppelt, um sofort als 'Anti-diver'-

Maschine eingesetzt werden zu können. **7** Pilot und Beobachter ein Mustang. Sie tragen 'Mae West' Lebens = rettungswesten, Sauerstoffmasken, Fliegerhelme und seidene Halstücher (als Nackenschutz beim ständigen Suchen nach feindlichen Flugzeugen). **8** Die Besatzung einer Mosquito mit zwei verschiedenen Fliegerstiefelmuster. **9** Spitfire Mk IXc Jagdflugzeuge von No. 349 (Belgian) Sqn, Friston, UK. **10** Die Tödliche Bewaffnung der Mosquito FB Mk IV.

11 & 12 Mosquitos greifen Marine-Ziele während einen Roadstead Einsatz gegen Schiffe an. **13** Diese Mosquito NF Mk XII von No. 29 Sqn, steht startbereit vor einem Nachteinsatz aus West Malling, UK. **14** Die erste Spitfire, die in Frankreich nach D-Day landete wird von RAF Servicing Commandos mit Treibstoff aus Behälter mittels eines Trichters besorgt. **15** Prefabricated Bitumised Strips (PBS) in einem Feldlager in Frankreich PBS wurde als unterlager für gelöcherte Stahlplatten benutzt. Dadurch wurde die schnelle Umwandlung einfacher Wiesen in Flugplätzen ermöglicht. **16** Ein Jagdpiloten-Briefing bei einem der ersten Ersatzflugplätze, die in Frankreich nach der Invasion in Anspruch genommen wurden. **17** Bodenbedienungspersonal bauen, mit Hilfe eines Krans, den Propellor einer Spitfire Mk IX ab. **18** Obwohl bid D-Day keine 'Frontmaschine' mehr, die Hurricane war immer noch in Einsatz; hier z.B. als Luftpostträger von UK nach Frankreich. **19** Eine Seafire Mk II wird durch den Schlamm eines Ersatzflugplatzes in der Kampfzone, kurz nach der Invasion, geleitet. **20** RAF Aircraftsman Hill eines Auster Beobachtungsstaffels trägt das Heeresärmelverbandsabzeichen der Heereseinheit der seine Staffel während des Invasionszeitabschnitt zugeteilt worden ist.

21 Eine mit Bomben beladene Spitfire Mk IXe. Unterm Propeller erscheint der Namenszug des Piloten; unterm Kanzel der Wimpel eines Wing Commanders. **22** Diese beschädigte Spitfire (laminierten, holzernen Propellor zerstört, Motoren- und Kanonenhauben entfernt) ist von einer RAF Bergungseinheit gerade zurückgeschleppt worden. **23** General Eisenhower nimmt eine mit Raketen bewaffnete Typhoon in Augenschein. **24** Vier Spitfire von No. 66 Sqn nach einem Einsatz indem sie zwei Fw 190s abgeschossen und vier weiteren beschädigt hatten. **25** Ein französisches Bauernhaus dient as Kantine für RAF Personal. **26** Funkgerätprüfung einer Mustang III, die AEAF Streifen und rot bemalte MG Mündungen hat. **27** Bewaffnete RAF Servicing Commandos auf einem Ersatzflugplatz in der vorderen Kampzone warten auf dem nächsten Jaboeinsatz mit Mustangs von No. 122 Sqn. **28** Diese Tempest V von No. 3 Sqn zeigt die schwarzweisse 'Invasionserkennungs streifen' alliierten Flugzeuge die sowohl vom Feinde als auch von den Alliierten Armeen wohl erkannt waren. **29** Motor-

feuerausbrüche waren mit der 'Napier Sabre' Motor der Typhoon gar nicht selten, deshalb bein Anlassen stand immer einen Mann mit Feuerbekämpfungsgerät dabei. **30** Um diesen Ersatzflugplatz glatt zu machen, ist diese Bauernwalze mit zwei 500lb Bomben beladen worden.

31 So klein der Mann! Er dient als Massstab für diese riesige Typhoon. **32** Panzerknacker! Typhoons werden mit panzerdurchbrechenden Raketen beladen. **33** Sogar bei solchem Schlamm flogen die Alliierten Piloten weiter—eine Typhoon, Frankreich. **34** Eine Spitfire Mk XIV mit 'Griffon' Motor, über Südengland, spät in 1943. **35** Eine Tempest V mit den Invasionserkennungsstreifen die auch von Typhoons, um möglichen Verwechslungen mit der Fw 190 zu verhindern, getragen wurden. **36** Ein Radwechsel mit einer Typhoon war manchmal haperig! **37** Diese Tempest trägt den Namenszug von Wing Cdr. Roland Beamont als Erkennungsbuchstaben und dazu unterm Kanzel, seinen Dienstgradwimpel. **38** Eine Tempest V von No. 501 Sqn Auxiliary Air Force, Hawkinge, UK, 1945. **39** Mosquitos greifen Schiffe by Porsgrunn, April 1945, an. **40** Spitfire Mk XIV, von Wing Cdr. Waddell, No. 39 Photo-reconnaissance Wing, Eindhoven, Januar 1945 geflogen. **41** Zwei Spitfire XIVs, Petit Bosel, Belgien 1945.

Farbtafeln

Seite 25: Offizierjagdpilot (Neuzeeländer) mit RAF 'Battledress' und dem später eingeführten Fliegerhelm, 'Mae West' Rettungsweste und 'Entkommungsstiefel', deren Wildlederschäfte abzumachen gingen. Piloten trugen oft Revolver in Blauen oder khakifärbigen Halftergürtel. Auf beinden Oberärmel ist das hell-oder dunkelblaue Hoheitszeichen angebracht. Die hell-oder dunkelblaue Dienstgradabzeichen sind als Schlaufen über die Schulterklappen überzogen worden.

Seite 26 Oben: Diese Spitfire Mk IXb, MK 826 von Nr. 412 Sqn wurde von Wing Cdr George Keefer, Juli 1944 aus Beny-sur-Mer, Douvres, Frankreich geflogen. Die vorschriftsmässigen Erkennungsbuchstaben (VZ) sind durch den Pilotennamenszug ersetzt worden. Die Tarnfarben sind für diesen Zeitabschnitt üblich— dunkelgrün, ozeangrau mit mittelseegrauen Unterseiten. Der Knauf und die Rumpfstreifen sind in himmelblauer Farbe; an den Flügelunterseiten sind die 18-inch Invasionserkennungsstreifen angebrachtworden. Der Dienstgradwimpel hat die Spitzen nach vorne (Steuerbordseite) bzw. nach hinten (Backbordseite). Erkennungsbuchstaben GC-K.

Seite 26 Unten: Tempest Mk V, NV706 von Nr. 486 Sqn, Volkel, Holland, Frühjahr 1945. Tarnfarben wie für die Spitfire, Knauf weiss, Erkennungsbuchstabe 'F' an beide Rumpfspitzenseiten. Himmelblauer Namenszug, schwarze Standnummer. Die Kokarde Typ 'B' an den Flügenoberflächen sind durch solche in Typ 'C' ersetzt worden. Das kleine Bild zeigt zwei 'Flying Bomb' Siegeszeichen unter dem Kanzel (nur an der Backbordseite).

Seite 27: Beaufighter Mk IF, V8324 von No. 29 Sqn, von Sqn Ldr Richards und Sgt Mills, Heimatflugplatz West Malling, Kent, UK 1942 geflogen. Anstrich schwarz mit Walt Disney 'Bambi und Thumper'—Emblem (nur an der Backbordseite) unterm Kanzel. Die beschädigte, und wieder ausgebesserte Flächen am Schwanzfloss sind etwas heller.

Seite 28–29: Typhoon Mk Ib, P7752 von No. 609 Sqn Auxiliary Air Force, von Sqn Ldr R. P. Beamont, Heimatflugplatz Manston, Kent, UK Nov '42–Juli '43 geflogen. Vorschriftsmässige RAF 'europäische' Tagesjagdflugzeug Tarnfarben mit himmelblauen Buchstaben und Knauf, letzteren mit roter Spitze. An den Flügelunterseiten die Typhoon/Tempest Erkennungsstreifen; an den Flügeloberseiten gelbe Streifen. Das persönliche Waffen (nur an der Steuerbordseite getragen): die weisse Rose (York) und zwei Jagdhörne über dem vielgebrauchten Wahlspruch 'TALLY HO' d.h. in RAF Volksmund 'Feindliche Flugzeuge angreifen!' Die Wörte gelb über die Siegestafel. Dienstgradwimpel zu beiden Seiten.

Seite 30: Mustang Mk III, FB353 von Nr. 314 (Polish) Sqn, Peterhead, Aberdeen, Schottland, November 1944. Das Tarnfarbenschema ist modofiziert Typ 'E', ozeangrau/mittelseegrau; Erkennungsbuchstaben himmelblau, Knauf und die ersten 30cm der Rumpfspitze weiss. (Letztere Erkennungsmerkmal für RAF Mustang IIIs). Flügelkokarden—oben Typ 'B'; unten Typ 'A'. Zuebeiden Seiten der Rumpfspitze das Polnische Hoheits-

zeichen unter dem Auspuffrohr. Die Siegestafel wurde nur an der Backbordseite getragen. Als 'anti-diver' eingesetzt vernichtete dieses Flugzeug sieben 'V-1s'. Die gelbe Vorderstreifen an den Flügeln von Maschinen, die gegen fliegenden Bomben eingesetzt wurden sind ab 17. August 1944 entferntworden. An manche Maschinen, die nachher auf Begleitdienst wiederversetzt wurden, wurden diese Streifen wiederangebracht.

Seite 31 Oben: Die persönlichen Abzeichen: (A) Flt. Sgt. A. M. L. Kennaugh, Tempest V, EJ 743, US-H von Nr. 56 Sqn. (B) Flg. Offr. R. 'Cheval' Lallament, Typhoon Mk Ib, Nr. 609 Sqn. (C) Typhoon DN 421, EL-C von Nr. 181 Sqn. (D) Cmdt. J. Schloesing, Spitfire Mk IX, BS 244, SW-P von Nr. 340 Sqn. (E) Sqn. Ldr. J. A. F. Maclachlan, Hurricane Mk IIc, BE 215, JX-1, No. 1 Sqn. (F) Flg. Offr. Rudd, Mosquito Mk II, DZ 706, P-YP, Nr. 23 Sqn.

Seite 31 Unten: Coles Crane Mk VII, series 7, Fabrikanstrich wie von der RAF 1942–45 eingesetzt. Einige Fahrzeuge/wurden khaki mit gelben Hakenteilen überstrichen. Die Fahrzeugnummer wurde in weiss auf die vordere Stossstange angebracht.

Seite 32 Links: Leading Aircraftsman, RAF Regiment 1943. Das Regiment wurde Februar 1942 für Flugplatzverteidigungsdienst errichtet. Die Uniform war Armeebattledress mit RAF Abzeichen. Die Feldausrüstung war in RAF blau-grauer oder Khakifarbe (wie hier) M 1937 mit Gasmaskenbehälter.

Seite 32 Recht: Airman 2nd Tactical Air Force, Holland, Winter 1944. Vorschriftsmässige RAF Schiffchen, Abzeichen aus messing, RAF Battledrass Bluse und Hosen mit 'Wellington'—stiefel. und Lederwams. Das Albatrosabzeichen (von allen RAF Mannschaften getragen) wurde auf beiden Schultern getragen.